The
HIDDEN PLACES
of
NORFOLK

including
the Norfolk Broads

Edited by
David Gerrard

Published by:
Travel Publishing Ltd
7a Apollo House, Calleva Park
Aldermaston, Berks, RG7 8TN

ISBN 1-902-00721-2
© Travel Publishing Ltd 1998

First Published:	*1989*	*Fifth Edition:*	*1998*
Second Edition:	*1993*		
Third Edition:	*1994*		
Fourth Edition:	*1996*		

Regional Titles in the Hidden Places Series:

Channel Islands	Cheshire
Cornwall	Devon
Dorset, Hants & Isle of Wight	Gloucestershire
Heart of England	Kent
Lake District & Cumbria	Lancashire
Norfolk	Northeast Yorkshire
Northumberland & Durham	Nottinghamshire
Peak District	Potteries
Somerset	South East
South Wales	Suffolk
Surrey	Sussex
Thames & Chilterns	Welsh Borders
Wiltshire	Yorkshire Dales

National Titles in the Hidden Places Series:

England	Ireland
Scotland	Wales

Printing by: Nuffield Press, Abingdon

Cartography by: Estates Publications, Tenterden, Kent

Line Drawings: Sarah Bird

Editor: David Gerrard

Cover : Clare Hackney

Born in 1961, Clare was educated at West Surrey College of Art and Design as well as studying at Kingston University. She runs her own private water-colour school based in Surrey and has exhibited both in the UK and internationally. The cover is taken from an original water-colour of Cley-next-the-Sea.

Foreword

The Hidden Places series is a collection of easy to use travel guides taking you, in this instance, on a relaxed but informative tour through Norfolk, a county famous for the Norfolk Broads but with a rich and interesting past, delightfu pastoral countryside and a beautiful coastline teeming with wildlife. Our books contain a wealth of interesting information on the history, the countryside, the towns and villages and the more established places of interest. But they also promote the more secluded and little known visitor attractions and places to stay, eat and drink many of which are easy to miss unless you know exactly where you are going.

We include hotels, inns, restaurants, public houses, teashops, various types of accommodation, historic houses, museums, gardens, garden centres, craft centres and many other attractions throughout Norfolk. Most places have an attractive line drawing and are cross-referenced to coloured maps found at the rear of the book. We do not award merit marks or rankings but concentrate on describing the more interesting, unusual or unique features of each place with the aim of making the reader's stay in the local area an enjoyable and stimulating experience.

Whether you are visiting the area for business or pleasure or in fact are living in the county we do hope that you enjoy reading and using this book. We are always interested in what readers think of places covered (or not covered) in our guides so please do not hesitate to use the reader reaction forms provided to give us your considered comments. We also welcome any general comments which will help us improve the guides themselves. Finally if you are planning to visit any other corner of the British Isles we would like to refer you to the list of other *Hidden Places* titles to be found at the rear of the book.

Contents

CHAPTER ONE
In and Around Norwich

The Cow Tower beside the River Wensum

Chapter 1 - Area Covered

For precise location of places please refer to the colour maps found at the rear of the book.

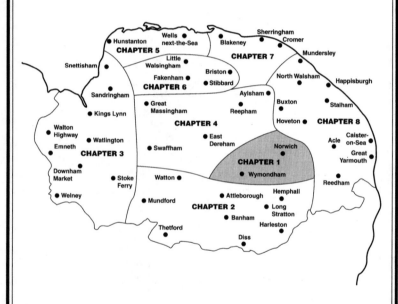

1
In & Around Norwich

Introduction

"Oh! rare and beautiful Norfolk" exclaimed John Sell Cotman, the gifted artist whose paintings and watercolours of heart-meltingly lovely scenes around the county in the early 1800s are amongst the greatest treasures of the County Museum in Norwich Castle. Then as now, Norfolk was a predominantly agricultural county with some 700 villages scattered across its 70-mile length and 40-mile breadth. Despite its ranking as the 4th largest of the English counties, Norfolk is listed 23rd in terms of population, a happy imbalance which results in great tracts of sparsely populated land, especially in the southwestern corner of the county.

Much more often quoted than Cotman's heartfelt cry is the glib remark by one of Noel Coward's characters: *"Very flat, Norfolk"*. It's true that the highest point in the county, near Cromer, only reaches 330ft above sea level, but this bare fact takes no account of the gentle undulations and sinuous country roads that create ever-changing views. It's not a dramatic landscape, but a subtle one which gradually insinuates itself into your favour, a land of soft pastures, abundant trees, and countless waterways, where everything is on a human scale.

And of all English counties, Norfolk is most notable for its endowment of a wealth of historic buildings: some 750 medieval churches, the ruins of 50 monasteries, hundreds of prehistoric and Roman remains, half a dozen of the stateliest homes in England, as well as thousands of interesting houses, cottages, barns and other buildings. The architectural historian Nikolaus Pevsner, compiling his monumental *"Buildings of England"* series, found it necessary to devote two books to this county rather than the usual single volume, and in Arthur Mee's comprehensive survey of *"The King's England"*, his book on Norfolk is the fattest of all the county tomes.

Norfolk owes this rich heritage to its prosperity during the Middle Ages when intensive agriculture and a thriving woollen trade greatly enriched its land-owning citizens. They in turn expressed their gratitude to the Divine Providence which had made them so wealthy by expending a moiety of their profits in funding the building of churches. Happily, these were the years when English ecclesiastical architecture was at its most inventive and ambitious: the medieval masons constructed buildings that were both sublime in scale and delicate in detail. In the following chapters, there is only space to notice the most remarkable of their creations: should you stop in the next village along the road from any of those included here, you will almost certainly find another church which, in a guide to any other county, would be assured of its own special mention.

Strange to say, Norfolk is actually an island, surrounded by sea to the north and east, isolated from Cambridgeshire by the River Great Ouse, and from Suffolk by the Little Ouse River and the River Waveney. Bulging out into the North Sea, the county is by-passed far away by the Great North Road, the A1, and there is still not a single mile of classified motorway within its boundaries. High-speed road travel in Norfolk is not an available option. That's a good thing in the opinion of many who believe that this is a county not to be rushed through, but to be savoured slowly, mile by mile.

Our survey of the county begins at one of the most likeable cities in England.

Norwich

"Norwich has the most Dickensian atmosphere of any city I know" declared J.B. Priestley in his *English Journey* of 1933. *"What a grand, higgledy-piggledy, sensible old place Norwich is!"* More than half-a-century later, in a European Commission study of *"most habitable"* cities, Norwich topped the list of British contenders, well ahead of more favoured candidates such as Bath and York. The political, social and cultural capital of Norfolk, Norwich has an individual charm which is difficult to define, a beguiling atmosphere created in part by its prodigal wealth of sublime buildings, partly by its intriguing dual personality as both an old-fashioned Cathedral town and a vibrant, modern metropolis.

Back in prehistoric times, there were several settlements around the confluence of the Rivers Wensum and Yare and, by the late fourth century, one of them was important enough to have its own mint. This was *Northwic* and by the time of the Domesday Book, 700 years later, Northwic/Norwich, had become the third most populous city in England, only outnumbered by London and York. To the Norman conquerors such a major centre of population (about 5,500 residents) needed a *Castle* to make sure its Saxon inhabitants were kept in order.

The first structure, in wood, was replaced in the late 1100s by a mighty fortress in stone which, unlike most blank-walled castles of the period, is decorated with a rich facade of blind arcades and ornamental pilasters. The great fort never saw any military action and as early as the 13th century it was being used as the county gaol, a role it continued to fill until 1889. From its walls, in December 1549, the leader of the rebellion against land enclosures, Robert Kett, was hung in chains and left to starve to death. The Castle is now a lively *Museum* where the old dungeons house a forbidding display of instruments of torture, along with the death masks of some of the prisoners who were executed here.

Norwich Castle

Amongst the countless other fascinating exhibits are the **Bulwer and Miller** collection of more than 2,600 English china teapots; the Langton collection of around 100 cats, fashioned in porcelain, ivory, bronze, glass, and wood, and originating from anywhere between Derbyshire and China; and Margaret Elizabeth Fountaine's mind-boggling accumulation of 22,000 butterflies which she had personally netted during her travels around the world. Pride of place must go however to the Museum's incomparable collection of paintings by the celebrated Norwich artist, John Sell Cotman (1782-1842), and others in the group known as the Norwich School. Their subjects were mostly landscape scenes, such as John Crome's *The Poringland Oak*, and quite apart from the artistic quality of their works, they have left a fascinating pictorial record of early 19th century Norfolk.

The Castle's function has changed over the years, but the **Cathedral** is still the focus of ecclesiastical life in the county. It's even older than the castle, its service of consecration taking place almost 900 years ago, in 1101. This peerless building, its flint walls clad in creamy-white stone from Caen is, after Durham, the most completely Norman cathedral in England, its appeal enhanced by later Gothic features such as the flying buttresses. The Norman cloisters are the largest in the country and notable for the 400 coloured and gilded bosses depicting scenes from medieval life. Another 1600 of these wondrous carvings decorate the glorious vaulted roof of the nave.

It's impossible to list all the Cathedral's treasures here, but do seek out the Saxon

Norwich Cathedral

Bishop's Throne in the Presbytery; the lovely 14th century altar painting in ***St Luke's Chapel***; and the richly carved canopies in the Choir.

Outside, beneath the slender 315ft high spire soaring heavenwards, the ***Cathedral Close*** is timeless in its sense of peace. There are some 80 houses inside the Close, some medieval, many Georgian, their residents enjoying an idyllic refuge free from cars. At peace here lie the remains of Nurse Edith Cavell. A daughter of the rector of Swardeston, a few miles south of Norwich, Nurse Cavell worked at a Red Cross hospital in occupied Brussels during World War I. She helped some 200 Allied soldiers to escape to neutral Holland before being detected and court-martialled by the Germans. As she faced execution by firing squad on 12 October 1915, she spoke her own resonant epitaph: *"Standing as I do, in the view of God and eternity, I realize that patriotism is not enough. I must have no hatred or bitterness towards anyone".*

A stroll around the Close will take you to ***Pull's Ferry*** with its picturesque flint gateway fronting the River Wensum. In medieval times, a canal ran inland from here so that provisions, goods, and in the earliest days, building materials, could be moved direct to the Cathedral. A short stroll along the riverside walk will bring you to ***Cow Tower***, built around 1378, and the most massive of the old city towers. And at the western end of the Cathedral Close is the magnificent ***Erpingham Gate***, presented to the city in 1420 by a hero of the Battle of Agincourt, Sir Thomas Erpingham.

Beyond this gate, in Tombland, (originally Toom- or waste-land), is ***Samson and Hercules House***, its entrance flanked by two 1674 carvings of the giants, and, diagonally opposite, the 15th century Maid's Head Hotel.

Cow Tower

7

About 400 yards to the west is the great open space of the Market Square where every weekday a colourful jumble of traders' stalls offer just about every conceivable item for sale. Dominating the western side of the market square is **City Hall**, modelled on Stockholm City Hall and opened by George VI in 1938. Opinions differ about its architectural merits, but there are no such doubts about its predecessor as Civic Centre, the nearby Guildhall, a fine example of 15th century flintwork which now houses the Tourist Information Centre and a small museum.

Just around the corner from City Hall, *The Alibi Wine Bar & Restaurant* in Bethel Street promises *"Great Music and Fabulous Food"* and, to judge by the lively atmosphere in this town centre restaurant, it delivers on its pledge. The restaurant is on two floors with the ground floor 36-seater restaurant serving a good choice of bar snacks, - a soup of the day, quiche, filled baguettes, ploughmans, smoked salmon & scrambled eggs, French bread pizza, along with hot meals and puddings listed on the board.

Children are welcome at this friendly restaurant, so there's also a menu specially for them. Upstairs, the à la carte menu offers more substantial meals such as Steak & Kidney Pie, Lasagne, potato Moussaka and a choice of French wines (including champagne) to accompany them.

With the Theatre Royal just a short walk away, The Alibi is also a favourite with theatre-goers looking for a pre- or post-performance supper. Benito Doynes, who runs this popular venue, also lays on music every weekday night. On

The Alibi Wine Bar & Restaurant

Mondays there's a jam session with the House Band when, if you're a student or musician, just buy a pint before 9 p.m. and a free meal comes with it. On other evenings, the live entertainment varies from day to day with leading groups playing anything from modern jazz to '70s Retro & Funk'. If you enjoy the great combination of live music and excellent food, this is definitely a restaurant to seek out. *The Alibi Wine Bar & Restaurant, 58, Bethel Street, Norwich, NR2 1NR. Tel: 01603 763188*

Running eastwards from the Guildhall is London Street where for more than 15 years **Linzers of London Street** has enjoyed an incomparable reputation for its superb cakes and pastries. Andrew Bell took the name of his very special café and pâtisserie from the Austrian treat, the Linzertorte, - sweet almond pastry with apricot jam. Other specialities of the house include Apple Strudel and Sachertorte, a rich chocolate sponge which is virtually Austria's National Cake!

Linzers has its own bakery and also specialises in wedding and celebration cakes, birthday, anniversary, and novelty cakes. You're welcome to go along and discuss your own ideas, - *"everything's pos-*

Linzers of London Street

sible" says Andrew. In the first floor licensed café, with its attractive cane chairs, stripped pine and ceiling fan, you face some very difficult choices between the Cream Teas, scones and the rich variety of other pâtisserie delights on offer. Linzers also serves an extensive choice of open or closed sandwiches, made with bread from their own bakery, as well as filled rolls, jacket potatoes, and generously heaped Salad Bowls offering such options as Feta Cheese with grapes and apricots. The menu also includes a good choice of savouries, (quiche of the day, or chilli pasty, for example), which are available either with just a garnish or with a full salad. Set in a quiet pedestrianised area, a sampling of the fare on offer at Linzers is an essential element of any visit to this historic city. *Linzers of London Street, 67, London Street, Norwich, NR2 1HL. Tel: 01603 630795*

One of Norwich's eating places which you should certainly seek out is **Lloyds of London Street**. You'll find it, naturally enough, in London Street. A dazzling display of hanging baskets and tubs of flowers frame the ground-floor entrance to this first-floor restaurant where your hosts are Hans Scherer and Martin Oxborrow. Cane-backed chairs, individual table lighting, and wood-clad walls hung with floral prints immediately suggest a Continental influence, an impression confirmed by a quick look at the menu. Amongst the starters there's a Smoked Salmon Rosti and the main courses include a Vienna Schnitzel and a Pastetli, - a hot vol-au-vent filled with meat mousse, gammon ham and mushrooms in a bouillon roux. The Pastetli recipe comes from Switzerland, as does Hans who is responsible for the exceptional cuisine on offer at this attractive restaurant.

Lloyd's of London Street

Along with his Swiss dishes, you'll also find a good choice of unmistakably English dishes, such as venison sausages and grilled gammon steak, as well as imaginative options like spinach & ricotta cheese strudel, and Chicken Casimir, - a poached chicken fillet served with a light curry and cream sauce. In good weather, you can eat alfresco in the pavement dining area. Although Lloyds of London Street only re-opened in May 1998, it already has a reputation that puts much longer-established restaurants in the shade. *Lloyds of London Street, 66, London Street, Norwich, NR2 1JT. Tel: 01603 624978*

Around the corner from London Street, in Bridewell Alley, is the **Bridewell Museum**, a late 14th century merchant's house now dedicated to Norfolk's crafts and industries. And right next door another museum/shop celebrates the county's great contribution to world cuisine, mustard. Back in the early 1800s, Jeremiah Colman perfected his blend of mustard flours and spice to produce a condiment that was smooth in texture and tart in flavour. Together with his nephew James he founded J & J Colman in 1823 and, a century and a half later, **The Mustard Shop** was established to commemorate the company's history. It also serves as a showcase for the range of Colman products which nowadays includes a variety of drinks and foods. The shop has an appropriately Victorian atmosphere with lots of mahogany and marble, and a fascinating display of vintage containers and advertisements, amongst them a series of cod detective stories featuring such characters as Lord Bacon of Cookham and Miss Di Gester, written by no less distinguished a writer than Dorothy L. Sayers. A very appetising exhibition.

There are still 32 churches in Norwich, all worth attention, although many are now used for purposes other than worship. Outstanding amongst them are **St Peter Mancroft**, a masterpiece of Gothic architecture built between 1430-55, and St Peter Hungate, a handsome 15th century church which, since 1933, has been a museum illustrating all aspects of the arts and crafts involved in ecclesiastical decoration and ritual. St Peter Hungate stands at the top of **Elm Hill**, a narrow, unbelievably picturesque lane where in medieval times the city's wool merchants built their homes, close to their warehouses beside the River Wensum.

The river crossing here is called **Fye Bridge** and nuzzling alongside the bridge, occupying a wonderful location overlooking the River Wensum, is **The Ribs of Beef**, one of Norwich's most historic inns. It was built in Elizabethan times as a private house and remained so until 1743. In that year, Thomas Holland converted it into an

The Ribs of Beef

alehouse and gave it the very 18th century, John Bull-ish name of
The Ribs of Beef.

Almost two centuries later, in 1928, a new landlord re-christened
the pub with the much less evocative "Fye Bridge Tavern". Happily,
when the present owners, Roger and Anthea Cawdron, took over in
1982 they restored the original name. Inside, the inn is furnished
and decorated in appropriately traditional style, with panoramic
windows overlooking the river where swans drift by in stately fash-
ion but won't hesitate to snap up any titbit thrown their way. Roger,
Anthea, their daughter Joolia and excellent staff offer a warm welcome to their patrons, efficient service, eleven cask conditioned guest
and permanent ales, (which have earned the inn an entry in the
CAMRA Good Beer Guide), a quality wine list, and excellent lunchtime food. This is available every day from 12 noon until 2.30pm on
weekdays, noon until 5.00pm at weekends, with special roasts &
puddings on Sundays, when booking is definitely recommended.

The menu offers a refreshingly varied choice of main meals and
light snacks, ranging from a Roast Norfolk Ham Salad to a jacket
potato filled with Cheddar & bacon; from a hearty home-made soup
to a Ribcracker Sandwich filled with juicy Sirloin Steak. The
"Wherryman's" Lunch Box is especially popular. Named after the

wherries, or black sail traders, that used to ply the river, the Lunch Box includes a generous wedge of mature Cheddar cheese and ripe Stilton teamed with a chunk of crusty bread and garnished with heaped helpings of coleslaw and garden-fresh salad. (Overnight riverborne patrons of The Ribs of Beef can take advantage of free mooring right outside). *The Ribs of Beef, Fye Bridge, Norwich, NR3 1HY. Tel: 01603 619517/Fax: 625446*

St Gregory's Church in Pottergate is another Norwich church to have been declared redundant, and its fate might well have been a sad one. Happily, it is now the home of the ***Saint Gregory's Trust***, a vibrant centre where local artists, actors, musicians, dancers, and other arts groups stage a variety of performances and exhibitions.

When the basic structure of the present church was built in the late 14th century, the general rule seems to have been that any parish of around 1000 people would have its own place of worship. St Gregory's was founded on the site of a Saxon church in 1210 and rebuilt in its present form in 1394. The church takes it name from Gregory the Great, the 6th century Pope best known for his campaign to convert the heathen Anglo-Saxons of Angle-land to Christianity. His enthusiasm for this mission, it's said, was fired by the sight of fair-haired youths from that distant country being paraded for sale in the Roman slave market. On being told that the captives were "Angles", he remarked that they were well-named, for they

Saint Gregory's Trust Arts, Music & Dance Centre

resembled angels. Impressed by their physical beauty, and pitying their ignorance of Christ's redemption, the Pope despatched a party of 40 monks to Angle-land in AD596, led by Augustine whom he consecrated as the first Archbishop of Canterbury.

Named after the missionary Pope, St Gregory's Church in Pottergate was later to become the most frequently-used church in the county for the purpose of sanctuary, the appealing medieval custom by which a fugitive from the savage laws of the time could seek refuge in a place of worship. This humane constraint on over-powerful feudal lords lasted from the late 4th century until its protection was abolished by James I in 1625. St Gregory's now offers a different kind of sanctuary, supporting and nurturing the artistic gifts of the city's creative people. *Saint Gregory's Trust, 15, Pottergate, Norwich, NR2 1DS. Tel: 01603 628777*

There can't be many architects who have added to their skills as a draughtsman by becoming adept with draught ale, but Mike Healy who, with Jo Cornish, runs the ***Rose Valley Tavern*** has done ex-

Rose Valley Tavern

actly that. Does his training as an architect, one wonders, make him itch to convert, knock-through, or generally re-assemble this handsome, double-fronted building with its panoramic windows? Mike, who arrived here in early 1998, insists that changes, if any, will be minimal. He likes the pub as it is, and so far his most outrageous innovations have been to bring in his dog, Arte, and to place a rug in front of the bar. *"Even that raised an eyebrow or two"* says Mike, but there were certainly no complaints when he and Jo introduced food to the Rose Valley at lunchtimes and evenings.

Their menu offers "pub grub" at its best, a wholesome choice that ranges from home-made soup of the day, to steak & kidney pies, omelettes, vegetarian options and much more. And, as a note on the menu points out, *"If it isn't listed, please ask - If we've got it, you can have it!"* Sundays at the Rose Valley Tavern are something rather special. Mike believes he has perfected a cure for the Sunday morning hangover. *"It's an English breakfast with coffee, served from 11 a.m., if I'm up by then"*. The day continues with Eric Clapton-style guitar playing in the afternoon and more live music in the evenings. This city-centre hostelry is also quite remarkable since it provides both disabled-friendly access and toilet, and a lawned area at the rear with a play area for children. And, a crucial amenity these days in such a busy city, the Rose Valley Tavern also offers its customers off-road parking. *Rose Valley Tavern, 111, Unthank Road, Norwich. Tel: 01603 626068*

Also located in the heart of the city, with museums, galleries, art centres and a wonderful shopping centre all within a few minutes walk, **The Woolpack**, as well as being an outstanding hostelry, is an interesting bygone structure, formerly the "town house" of the Walsingham Priors. The inside of this historic pub has been lately

The Woolpack

renewed by an interior designer, and the ambience now is one of a comfortable cafe bar within the environment of an ancient inn. Beams and a big old log fire dominate. There's also an attractive courtyard, overlooking a churchyard and surrounded by mature trees, - unusual for a city centre pub. In fine weather, the courtyard provides a favourite lunch-time and early evening rendezvous for people gathering to sit and chat, and enjoy a beer or two.

The food at The Woolpack is a fantastic combination of the innovative and the more orthodox, - if it's ordinary pub grub you are looking for, you won't find it here! The inn's reputation for superb food is well-merited, with vegetarian dishes and meals for special diets adding to the choices. The wines, too, are awfully good. A specialist importer supplies The Woolpack and excellent wines from all over the world are listed at affordable prices. Three or four ales are always on tap, and almost all the leading brands of keg and bottled beers are available. The Woolpack's cosmopolitan crowd of regular patrons create a very special atmosphere, a mood enhanced by the efficient and friendly staff who always put the customer first. Three beautiful letting rooms make the inn a perfect place to stay when you visit Norwich, with residents' parking as an additional amenity.

Open all day, seven days a week, The Woolpack is a unique place to enjoy food, whether it's lunch, supper, or a snack at any time. If you're not hungry, just sit, relax, and enjoy a pleasant drink at this pub that feels as though it belongs alongside a village green, but in fact is set in the heart of one of England's finest cities. *The Woolpack, Muspole Street, Norwich. Tel: 01603 611139*

On the western edge of the city stands the **University of East Anglia**. It's well worth making your way here to visit the **Sainsbury Centre for Visual Arts**. Housed in a huge hall of aluminium and glass designed by Norman Foster, the Centre contains the eclectic collection of a "passionate acquirer" of art, Sir Robert Sainsbury. For more than 50 years, Sir Robert purchased whatever works of art took his fancy, ignoring fashionable trends and "correct" choices. So you'll find sculptures and pictures by Henry Moore, Bacon and Giacometti, along with African and pre-Columbian artefacts; Egyptian, Etruscan and Roman bronzes; works by Indians and by Inuit eskimos; sculptures from the Cyclades, the South Seas, the Orient and medieval Europe. This extraordinary collection was donated to the University by Sir Robert and Lady Lisa Sainsbury in 1973; their son David complemented his parents' generosity by paying for the building in which it is housed.

To the south of Norwich are the remains of **Venta Icenorum**, the Roman town established here after Boadicea's rebellion in AD 61. Unusually, this extensive site has not been disturbed by later developments, so archaeologists have been able to identify the full scale of the original settlement. Sadly, very little remains above ground, although in dry summers the grid pattern of the streets show up as brown lines in the grass. Most of the finds discovered during excavations in 1920s and 30s are now in **Norwich Castle Museum**, but the riverside site is still worth visiting, especially if you have a vivid imagination.

Around Norwich

Poringland   *Map 5 ref J7*
6 miles SE of Norwich, on the B1332

This sizeable village is surrounded by mustard fields, a dazzling sight in June when the custard-coloured blooms create a cloth of gold and, according to old folk lore, their glow shines all the way up to the moon. The name of the village will be familiar to those who love the paintings of the Norwich artist John Crome (1794-1842) whose arcadian painting of *The Poringland Oak* hangs in the Tate Gallery.

Fortunately, **Old Grumpy's** in Poringland is one of those pubs that doesn't live up to its name. It isn't clear who the original old grump was but he certainly wouldn't fit in nowadays at this lively,

Old Grumpy's

friendly pub/restaurant owned and run by Christina Tasker. Christina took over in 1995, refurbished the interior in a pleasing decor of light oak, and overhauled the menu. The restaurant is separate from the two bars and serves an excellent choice of "Old Grumpy's Gastronomic Delights". Amongst the starters, there's a wonderful dish of Baked Broadland Mushrooms in a tomato, cream, & parsley sauce, topped with a parmesan crust. The main course menu offers fish, steaks, meat and vegetarian choices, while lovers of traditional desserts will be pleased to see listed an individual bread & butter pudding served with apricot sauce. Food is available every lunchtime and evening, and business breakfasts are also served. The restaurant at Old Grumpy's can be booked for receptions and functions. In the bar, there's a large screen TV for sport as well as a pool table and darts board. Unusually for a pub, Old Grumpy's even has its own bowling green and a team which has achieved great success in the various County leagues. Take them on at your peril! *Old Grumpy's, 119, The Street, Poringland, NR14 7RP. Tel: 01508 492420*

To the southwest of Poringland is **The Playbarn**, an indoor and outdoor adventure centre specially designed for the under-sevens. All the play equipment is based on a farmyard theme with a miniature farm, bouncy tractors, soft play sheep pens, and donkey rides among the attractions. Refreshments and light lunches are available, or you can bring along your own picnic, and The Playbarn's unusual pricing policy requires that only children pay for admission: adult entry is free. The centre is open daily all year, except on Saturdays. For more details, telephone 01508 495526.

Swainsthorpe
6 miles S of Norwich, on the A140

Map 5 ref J7

On the outskirts of Swainsthorpe, the parish church is notable for its circular Norman tower, crowned with a 14th century belfry. For gardeners from all across East Anglia, however, Swainsthorpe has a different attraction and they regularly make their way to this small village for the express purpose of visiting **Lodge Farm Nurseries**. Roger and Patricia Young established the nurseries some 16 years ago and they have gone from strength to strength, earning a solid

Lodge Farm Nurseries

reputation for healthy, top-quality plants, shrubs and trees. The 5-acre growing area includes many unusual plants and shrubs, including a good selection of specimens. In the spring, Lodge Farm Nurseries will also create hanging-baskets to order from a huge variety of trailing plants. The well-laid out grounds are a pleasure to wander around, with many attractive displays to admire. The nurseries are open 7 days a week and the well-informed staff are always happy to assist with any gardening needs or problems you may have. *Lodge Farm Nurseries, Brick Kiln Lane, Swainsthorpe, NR14 8PY. Tel: 01508 471104*

Wreningham   Map 5 ref I8
8 miles SW of Norwich, on the B1113

From the outside, only the hanging sign betrays the fact that ***The Bird in Hand*** is a freehouse and restaurant. Otherwise, the impressive old house with walls of warm red brick and a well-stocked garden gives every impression of simply being a very desirable private residence. The Bird in Hand is owned and run by Carol Turner who, in the ten years she has been here, has received numerous plaudits for the quality of the food on offer. One, which is framed and hangs in the entry foyer, came from the trade magazine "Publican" which rated the Bird in Hand as the 2nd Best Restaurant in England.

The Bird in Hand

In fact, there are actually two restaurants here: one furnished and decorated in an elegant Victorian style, the other resembles a traditional farmhouse setting. The same excellent food, however, is available in either. Carol trained at catering college so all her dishes are freshly prepared from top quality ingredients. The à la carte menu, which changes daily, offers a wide choice that ranges from steaks, (served if you wish with the Bird in Hand's own wild mushroom, black pepper and sherry sauce), to a vegetarian lasagne. Daily Specials extend the choice even further. The scrumptious desserts include a home-made Cheesecake of the Day and a wonderful Summer Fruits Bread Pudding.

Food is also available in the bar, an attractive room with tiled floor and open beams. There's a huge choice of meals on offer, - filled, freshly baked baguettes, jacket potatoes, vegetarian options, as well as hearty dishes like the Bird in Hand's own steak, kidney and field mushroom pie. Weather permitting, you can also enjoy your refreshments in the peace of the landscaped beer gardens at the rear of the house. If you are anywhere in the area, then the Bird in Hand should definitely be sought out. *The Bird in Hand, Wreningham, NR16 1BW. Tel: 01508 489438*

Wymondham   Map 5 ref I7
9 miles SW of Norwich, off the A11

The exterior of **Wymondham Abbey** presents one of the oddest ecclesiastical buildings in the county; the interior reveals one of the most glorious. The Abbey was founded in 1107 by the Benedictines, or Black Friars, as they were known from the colour of their habits. The richest and most aristocratic of the monastic orders, the Black Friars apparently experienced some difficulty in respecting their solemn vows of poverty and humility. Especially the latter.

The monks were constantly in conflict with the people of Wymondham. In 1249, the dissension between them was so bitter that Pope Innocent IV himself attempted to reconcile their differences. When his efforts failed, a wall was then built across the interior of the Abbey, dividing it into an area for the monks and another for the parishioners. Even that drastic measure failed to bring peace. Both parties wanted to ring their own bells, so each built a tower. The villagers erected a stately rectangular tower at the west end; the monks an octagonal one over the crossing, thus creating the Abbey's curious exterior appearance. Step inside however and you find a magnificent Norman nave, 112ft long. (It was originally twice as long, but the eastern end, along with most of the Abbey buildings, was demolished after the Dissolution of the Monasteries).

The superb hammerbeam roof is supported by 76 beautifully carved angels; there's an interesting 16th century tomb, of the last Abbot, in delicate terracotta work; and a striking modern memorial, a gilded and coloured reredos and tester, commemorating the local men who lost their lives in World War I.

The rectangular western tower of the Abbey was the setting for one of the last acts in the ill-fated Kett's Rebellion of 1549. From its walls, William Kett was hung in chains and left to die: his brother, Robert, the leading figure in the uprising, suffered the same fate at Norwich Castle.

Although many of Wymondham's oldest houses were lost in the fire of 1615 when some 300 dwellings were destroyed, there are still some attractive Elizabethan buildings in the heart of the town. **The Market Place** is given dignity by the picturesque octagonal Market Cross, rebuilt two years after the fire. Crowned by a pyramid roof, this appealing timber-framed building is open on all sides on the ground floor, and its upper floor is reached by an outside stairway. Also of interest is **Becket's Chapel**, founded in 1174 and restored in 1559. In its long history it has served as a pilgrim's chapel, grammar school, and coal store. Currently, it houses the town library. **The Bridewell**, or House of Correction, in Bridewell Street, was built as a model prison in 1785 along lines recommended by the prison reformer, John Howard, who had condemned the earlier gaol on the site as "one of the vilest in the country". Wymondham's Bridewell is said to have served as a model for the penitentiaries established in the United States. Now owned by the town's Heritage Society, Bridewell is home to several community projects, including the **Wymondham Heritage Museum**.

Railway buffs will also want to visit the historic **Railway Station**, built in 1845 on the Great Eastern's Norwich-Ely line. At its peak, the station and its section employed over 100 people. Still providing a rail link to Norwich, London and the Midlands, the station has been restored, and its buildings house a railway museum, restaurant and tea room, and a piano showroom.

Not all that long ago, the 5000 or so residents of this handsome market town sustained no fewer than 48 pubs, taverns, inns, alehouses, gin-shops, vintners and sundry other sources of alcoholic solace. In those days of what was, one imagines, a very Merry England, Wymondham was providing about one watering-hole for every ten inhabitants. **The Queens Head**, in the heart of the town, is one of the great survivors of those sociable times. The building itself dates back to the early 1700s, so the monarch after whose head it was named was probably Queen Anne who reigned from 1702 until 1714. Lesley Smith took over here in early 1998, spent something like £30,000 on refurbishing and upgrading the ancient inn's amenities, and now finds herself as host to the town's most popular hostelry. There are several good reasons for this popularity. There's Lesley herself and her daughter who both welcome visitors with genuine warmth; there's an ambience in which both children, the Round Table, and business conferences can feel equally at ease; and a menu which is remarkable for its freshness of style and its extraordinary value for money. The varied menu includes fresh baguettes, (filled with ham off the bone, or hot beef and horseradish, for example). A Chilli Crock Pot; and a hearty, traditional Sausage & Mash are always featured, along with a vegetarian Leek & Cheese Crumble, as well as a further choice of daily

The Queens Head

specials. Children have their own menu. Every weekday there's also a Senior Citizens' 2-course menu, and on Sundays, The Queen's Head serves a very special 2-course lunch which should not be missed. Ale lovers, by the way, will be delighted to know that the inn stocks no fewer than six real ales. *The Queens Head, 2, Bridewell Street, Wymondham, NR18 0AR. Tel: 01953 602345*

Suton

Map 5 ref H8

12 miles SW of Norwich, on minor road off the A11

Children especially enjoy farmhouse holidays and they will be in their element at **Rose Farm**, Joy and Douglas Durrant's warm and friendly bed and breakfast establishment. Situated on the outskirts of the village, Rose Farm stands in 8 acres of open pasture land where ducks, geese and chickens have free range to wander. The three donkeys, Joy's special pets, are always particularly popular with visitors. The farmhouse itself is some 300 years old and was Douglas' original family home. It was converted into bed and break-

Rose Farm

fast accommodation in 1980, with all modern amenities provided. There are four well-appointed guest rooms, all conveniently located on the ground floor. All the rooms have television and teamaking facilities, and both a bathroom and a shower room are available. Rose Farm is open all year (apart from Christmas and New Year), and everyone is welcome: children, smokers, dogs too. For anyone planning to explore central Norfolk, the farm is well-positioned. Wymondham Abbey and the Tropical Butterfly Centre at Attleborough are both close by, Norwich with its multitude of attractions is just a dozen miles away, and in less than an hour you can drive to the sandy beaches of the east Norfolk coast. *Rose Farm, School Lane, Suton, nr Wymondham, NR18 9JN. Tel: 01953 603512*

CHAPTER TWO
Breckland and South Norfolk

Bressingham Steam Museum

Chapter 2 - Area Covered

For precise location of places please refer to the colour maps found at the rear of the book.

2
Breckland & South Norfolk

Breckland

"Drie, barren and miserably sandy" was John Evelyn's impression of Breckland in 1667, adding that it reminded him of *"the sands in the deserts of Libya"*. The following year, the village of Santon Downham was completely smothered by a sand-storm that blew in from the wastes of Breckland in a 10-mile wide band, temporarily choking the River Little Ouse as well. Even today, if you ask a farmer whether his land lies in Norfolk or Suffolk, he may well respond *"Depends on which way the wind's blowing"*.

The reason for this outlandish phenomenon is that Breckland, which extends for more than 940 sq. km. in southwest Norfolk and northwest Suffolk, is underlain by chalk with only a light covering of soil. The name "Breckland" comes from the dialect word, breck, meaning an area of land which was cultivated for a while, then allowed to revert to heath after the poor soil had become exhausted.

The problem had its origins in the Neolothic farmers who some 6000 years earlier felled the scrubby trees that once covered the area. The lack of replanting meant that the thin soils could only sustain heathland. It wasn't until the early 1800s AD that large-scale planting of trees was undertaken, a process vastly expanded in the 1920s by the Forestry Commission. It's possible to see how Breckland used to look by visiting the East Wretham Heath Nature Reserve, northeast of Thetford. There are nature trails here, hides for watching the birds and deer, and an abundance of wild flowers. Admission is free.

Thetford

Some 2000 years ago, Thetford may well have been the site of **Boadicea's Palace**. In the 1980s, excavations for building development at Gallows Hill, north of the town, revealed an Iron Age enclosure. It is so extensive it may well have been the capital of the Iceni tribe which gave the Romans so much trouble. Certainly, the town's strategic location at the meeting of the Rivers Thet and Little Ouse made it an important settlement for centuries. At the time of the Domesday Book, 1086, Thetford was the sixth largest town in the country and the seat of the Bishop of East Anglia, with its own castle, mint and pottery.

Of the **Castle**, only the 80ft motte remains, but it's worth climbing to the top of this mighty mound for the views across the town. An early Victorian traveller described Thetford as *"An ancient and princely little town....one of the most charming country towns in England"*. Despite major development all around, the heart of the

Thetford Priory

town still fits that description, with a goodly number of medieval and Georgian houses presenting an attractive medley of flint and half-timbered buildings. Perhaps the most striking is the **Ancient House Museum** in White Hart Street, a magnificent 15th century timber-framed house with superb carved oak ceilings. It houses the Tourist Information Centre and a museum where some of the most interesting exhibits are replicas of the Thetford Treasure, a 4th-century hoard of gold and silver jewellery discovered as recently as 1979 by an amateur archaeologist with a metal detector. The originals of these sumptuous artefacts are housed in the British Museum. Admission to the museum is free, except during July and August when a small charge is made.

Even older than the Ancient House is the 12th century **Cluniac Priory** (English Heritage), now mostly in ruins but with an impressive 14th century gatehouse still standing. During the Middle Ages, Thetford could boast 24 churches, today only three remain.

Thetford's industrial heritage is vividly displayed in the **Burrell Steam Museum**, in Minstergate, which has full-size steam engines regularly "in steam", re-created workshops and many examples of vintage agricultural machinery. The Museum tells the story of the Burrell Steam Company which formed the backbone of the town's industry from the late 18th to the early 20th centuries, their sturdy machines famous around the world.

In King Street, the Thomas Paine Statue commemorates the town's most famous son, born here in 1737. The revolutionary philosopher, and author of "The Rights of Man", emigrated to America in 1774 where he helped formulate the American Bill of Rights. Paine's democratic views were so detested in England that even ten years after his death in New York State, the authorities refused permission for his admirer, William Cobbett, to have the remains buried in his home country. And it wasn't until the 1950s that Thetford finally got around to erecting a statue in his honour. Ironically for such a robust democrat, his statue stands in King Street and opposite **The King's House**, named after James I who was a frequent visitor here between 1608 and 1618. At the Thomas Paine Hotel in White Hart Street, the room in which it is believed that Paine was born is now the Honeymoon Suite, complete with four-poster bed.

To the west of the town stretch the 90 square miles of **Thetford Forest**, the most extensive lowland forest in Britain. The Forestry Commission began planting in 1922 and although the woodland is largely given over to conifers, with Scots and Corsican Pine and

Douglas Fir predominating, oak, sycamore and beech can also be seen throughout. There is a particularly varied trail leading from the Forestry Commission Information Centre which has detailed information about this and other walks through the area.

On the edge of the forest, about 2 miles west of Thetford, are the ruins of **Thetford Warren Lodge**, built around 1400. At that time a huge area here was preserved for farming rabbits, a major element of the medieval diet. The vast warren was owned by the Abbot of Thetford Priory and it was he who built the Lodge for his gamekeeper. Still in the forest, reached by a footpath from the village of Santon Downham, are **Grimes Graves** (English Heritage), the earliest major industrial site to be discovered in Europe. At these unique Neolithic flint mines, Stone Age labourers extracted the materials for their sharp-edged axes and knives. It's a strange experience entering these 4000 year old shafts which descend some 30ft to an underground chamber. (The experience is even better if you bring your own high-powered torch).

Mundford
Map 4 ref E8

8 miles NW of Thetford, on the A1065/A134

Mundford is a large Breckland village of flint built cottages, set on the northern edge of Thetford Forest and with the River Wissey running by. Overlooking the village green is **The Crown Hotel**. A curious feature of The Crown is that, in this so-called "flat" county, the hotel is built into a hill. You can equally walk in on level ground to the bars and to the first floor restaurant, - particularly helpful for disabled guests. This charming hotel has a history going back to 1652. It was originally built as a hunting lodge and later became the only hostelry on the vast Lynford Estate.

The Crown Hotel

For many years, the inn also played host to the local magistrates with a court being held here every second Tuesday. And until fairly recently, what is now the Old Court Restaurant was used as a Doctor's waiting room. It's been said that because of poor sound insulation on the door, it was very common to actually hear the doctor's diagnosis of the patient before you! Barry Walker is the resident proprietor of this outstanding hotel where informality is the order of the day, and there's a huge emphasis on 'good old-fashioned hospitality'. Barry believes that The Crown's reputation has flourished by providing interesting food, using produce from mainly local sources, and by listening to guests' comments about the results. The varied food on offer includes a regularly changing à la carte menu, a daily specials board, a "pub fayre" menu, - and the chef's flair if you have any special requests or dietary requirements. There are two dining-rooms: the Old Court Restaurant steeped in tradition, with bare floorboards, rugs and impromptu tables, and the Club Dining Room for more informal occasions.

The two bars are furnished in contrasting styles: choose either the peaceful Squire's Bar or the traditional Village Bar. The Crown has 16 letting rooms, from a good old-fashioned Four Poster Room, to twin and single rooms. All rooms are en suite. Whether you come for just a tipple, a meal, or an overnight stay, a visit to The Crown is an absolute must for anyone in the area. *The Crown Hotel, Crown Road, Mundford, Thetford, IP26 5HQ. Tel: 01842 878233*

If you ever watch television, you've almost certainly seen **Lynford Hall**, a mile or so northwest of Mundford. It has provided an impressive location for scenes in *"Dad's Army"*, *"Allo, Allo"*, *"You Rang My Lord"*, and *"Love on a Branch Line"*, as well as featuring in numerous television commercials. The Hall is a superb Grade II listed mansion, built for the Lyne-Stevens family in 1885, (as a hunting-

Lynford Hall

lodge, incredibly), and designed in the Jacobean Renaissance style by William Burn. At that time, the Lyne-Stevens estate included the whole of Thetford Forest and even today the Hall's present owners, The Organic Group Ltd., retain some 27 acres, with access to a further 500 acres of parkland. The Organic Group acquired Lynford Hall estate in March 1997, and have spent lavishly on transforming this magnificent building into East Anglia's premier conference, banqueting and exhibition venue. The Lyne-Stephens and William Burn function suites offer ample space for up to 500 guests, and for those who wish to stay overnight, parts of the Hall and its former stables, arranged around several attractive courtyards, are available for accommodation.

Lynford Hall has been granted a licence for the solemnisation of marriages and its superlative setting has made it one of the region's most popular venues for weddings. The ceremony can be held in any of the function rooms, (although some betrotheds opt for the gardens), and the lovely surroundings provide perfect photo-opportunities for the wedding portfolio. There are formal Italian gardens, a lake, and a Roman sunken garden with a bubbling well. Just a short walk away an 18th century gazebo, *"The Temple of Mercury"*, enjoys views across the lawns to a Japanese water garden and Tea House. And by the time you read this, The Organic Group may well have completed its plans to operate as a 4-Star Hotel with an elegant 80-cover restaurant overlooking those colourful Italian gardens. *Lynford Hall, nr Mundford, Thetford, IP26 5HW. Tel: 01842 878351/Fax: 878252*

Thompson
Map 4 ref F8

10 miles NE of Thetford, on minor road off the A1075

This is a quiet village with a marshy man-made lake, **Thompson Water**, and a wild common. **The Peddars Way** long-distance footpath passes about a mile to the west and, about the same distance to the north-east, the Church is a splendid early-14th century building notable for its fine carved screen and choice 17th century fittings.

The Chequers Inn at Thompson is indescribably pretty. With its thatched roof swooping almost to the ground, white-painted walls and multitude of colourful hanging-baskets, it presents the kind of picture that used to appear on chocolate box covers. The interior of this 17th century building is equally charming, with exposed timber beams that are even older than the house (possibly 14th century), low ceilings whose height varies unpredictably from room to room, and an abundance of gleaming brasses and other vintage agricultural bygones.

The Chequers Inn

Heather and Richard McDowall arrived at this idyllic old inn early in 1998 and have added to its many attractions by providing an excellent choice of wholesome, carefully prepared and presented food. Richard is the chef and his varied menu ranges from freshly-baked filled baguettes to hearty 12oz steaks; from appetising starters such as his own Chicken Liver Pâté, through a vegetarian selection and a children's menu to a wonderfully indulgent choice of desserts. In addition, on the specials' board you'll find a wide variety of fresh fish dishes to choose from. A choice of four Real Ales, a beer garden, and a safe, secluded children's play area all help to confirm one's feeling that at The Chequers one has finally found the ideal English pub. *The Chequers Inn, Griston Road, Thompson, Thetford, IP24 1PX. Tel/Fax: 01953 483360*

Watton   *Map 4 ref F7*
14 miles NE of Thetford, on the A1075

Watton's striking town sign depicts the *"Babes in the Wood"* of the famous nursery story. The story, which was already current hereabouts in the 1500s, relates that as Arthur Truelove lay dying, he decided that the only hope for his two children was to leave them in the care of their uncle. Unfortunately, the uncle decided to help himself to their inheritance and paid two men to take the children into nearby **Wayland Wood** and kill them. In a moment of unexpected compassion, one of the men decided that he could not commit the dastardly act. He disposed of his accomplice instead and abandoned the children in the wood to suffer whatever fate might befall them. Sadly, unlike the nursery tale in which the children find their way back home and live happily ever after, this unfortunate brother and sister perished. Their ghosts are said to wander hand in hand through the woods to this day.

Wayland Wood is now owned by the Norfolk Naturalist Trust and is believed to be one of the oldest in England; **Griston Hall** (private), half a mile south of the wood, is a Grade II listed building, reputedly the home of the Wicked Uncle in the Babes in the Wood story.

Watton itself is a rather drab little town but it does boast an unusual **Clock Tower**, dated 1679, standing at the centre of its long main street.

Rockland St Peter *Map 5 ref G8*
15 miles NE of Thetford, on the B1077

The main building of historical interest in this straggling village is its church with a round Norman tower and thatched roof, but Rockland St Peter is better known to East Anglian gardeners who seek it out in order to visit the **Walnut Tree Garden Nursery**. Set in a tranquil corner of the Norfolk heartland, the nursery is a small family-run business committed to giving its customers a wide choice of top quality garden plants.

Jim Paine and Clare Billington took over here in early 1998, and they grow many of their own plants, especially herbaceous perennials. There's an extensive selection to choose from, many of them unusual or only infrequently offered for sale, and thus hard to find. Because customers are buying direct from a working nursery, where much of the stock is grown on site, they can be confident of getting

Walnut Tree Garden Nursery

excellent quality and value. In time, visitors will be able to enjoy the nursery gardens that Jim and Claire are developing. These will illustrate different planting schemes, colour co-ordination, the passing of the seasons, and the interplay of foliage, flowers and fruit. The gardens will form a "living catalogue" of the plants the Nursery grows and sells.

As well as the ever increasing number of herbaceous perennials, the Walnut Tree also offers a wide selection of both ornamental and fruit trees, shrubs, roses, climbers, and alpines. And if the particular specimen you are seeking is not in stock, Jim and Clare pride themselves on the efforts they make to track these down and to ensure you get precisely the plant you are looking for. *Walnut Tree Garden Nursery, Flymoor Lane, Rockland St Peter, NR17 1BP. Tel: 01953 488163/Fax:483187/e-mail: jimnclare@aol.com*

Attleborough   Map 5 ref H8
16 miles SW of Norwich, off the A11

The greatest glory of this pleasant market town is to be found in its **Church of St Mary**. Here, a remarkable 15th century chancel screen stretches the width of the church and is beautifully embellished with the arms of the 24 bishoprics into which England was divided at that time. The screen is generally reckoned to be one of the most outstanding in the country, a remarkable survivor of the Reformation purging of such beautiful creations from churches across the land.

Collectors of curiosities will be interested in a strange memorial in the churchyard. It takes the form of a pyramid, about 6ft high, and was erected in 1929 to mark the grave of a local solicitor with the rather splendid name of Melancthon William Henry Brooke, or "Lawyer" Brooke as he was more familiarly known. Melancthon was an amateur Egyptologist who became convinced by his studies of the Pharoahs' tombs that the only way to ensure an agreeable afterlife was to be buried beneath a pyramid, precisely placed, and of the correct physical dimensions. Several years before his death, he gave the most punctilious instructions as to how this assurance of his immortal existence should be constructed and located.

A couple of miles west of Attleborough, the **Tropical Butterfly Gardens and Bird Park** is set in 2400 square feet of landscaped tropical gardens and provides a congenial home for hundreds of exotic tropical butterflies. There's also a Falconry Centre with flying displays twice daily; 1½ miles of paths and a waterside walk; a 2-acre Garden Centre with more than 2000 plant varieties on offer; a gift shop; coffee shop and tea gardens. Tel: 01953 453175.

East Harling
Map 5 ref G9

8 miles NE of Thetford, on the B1111

This attractive little town boasts a beautiful 15th century church in a pastoral location beside the River Thet. Inside, a magnificent hammer-beam roof crowns the lofty nave, there's some outstanding 15th century glass, and in the Harling Chapel, the fine marble ***Tomb of Robert Harling***.

Harling was one of Henry V's knights who met his death at the siege of Paris in 1435. Since this was long before the days of refrigeration, the knight's body was instead stewed, then stuffed into a barrel, and brought back to East Harling for a ceremonious burial.

Tomb of Sir Thomas Lovell

The church houses another, equally sumptuous memorial, the ***Tomb of Sir Thomas Lovell***. Sculpted in alabaster, Sir Thomas is an imposing figure, clad in armour with a long sword, his head resting on a helmet, his feet on a spray of peacock's feathers. He and his wife lie beneath a wondrously ornamented canopy, decorated with multi-coloured shields and pinnacles.

Located in the heart of this appealing little market town is ***The Nags Head***, owned and run by Glynis and Jim Clark, both of whom have long experience as licensees. Glynis is also well-known for her interest in Weimaraner dogs, a breed which originated in Weimar, Germany. Glynis breeds them part-time, and Jim trains them as gun dogs. Another of Jim's interests is collecting militaria. Behind the bar you'll see a fascinating collection of Army, Navy, and Air Force badges and caps from both officers and other ranks.

But The Nags Head is perhaps best known for its excellent food, prepared from prime ingredients by Glynis. Bar meals are available every lunchtime and evening, and at weekends there's also an à la carte menu and a traditional Sunday lunch. The bar menu offers a good choice of fish, meat and vegetable dishes, with some really tasty home-made offerings: Chicken, Ham & Mushroom Pie for example, or Piquant Pork, - succulent pork casseroled with peppers in a mustard and white wine sauce. There's always a home-made Soup of the Day and the freshly prepared desserts are listed on a blackboard. (On good weather days, you can enjoy your meal on the large patio outside where there's a lovely pergola draped with hanging baskets of flowers). The weekend à la carte menu includes some

The Nags Head

very tempting options: Avocado Ogenale as your starter perhaps, with a Venison Ragout or Chinese Money Bags to follow.

From time to time Glynis also arranges theme nights when all the dishes are drawn from the cuisine of one particular country. While you are in East Harling, you should have a look at its church which boasts a magnificent hammer-beam roof, perhaps the finest in East Anglia, and at the old windmill on the edge of the town.

Other attractions nearby include Swallow Aquatics, Snetterton Motor Racing Course, and the Forest Walk through West Harling Heath. *The Nags Head, Market Street, East Harling, NR16 2AD. Tel: 01953 718140*

Just outside the village, delightfully set at the edge of Thetford forest in a quiet corner of Roudham Farm, is ***Dolphin Lodge***. These two semi-detached cottages are ideal for a relaxing country holiday in the beautiful Breckland countryside. They were recently rebuilt by the farm's owners, Tim and Ellen Jolly, who took great care to retain many traditional features, - beams, natural wood, and inglenook fireplaces. Both cottages are extremely spacious, with large kitchens and living rooms, and fully equipped with amenities that range from central heating, through washing machines and tumbler driers to collections of books and games. In addition, East Dolphin cottage has an electric Aga and a jacuzzi bath.

Dolphin Lodge

The accommodation in both cottages comprises one double and one family room. Children of all ages are welcome, but for practical reasons no pets are allowed and no smoking is preferred. Dolphin Lodge is set in a large and safe garden, equipped with a climbing frame and surrounded by mature trees, where each morning you may see other local residents - pheasants, deer, rabbits and squirrels.

Next to the cottages, a former double garage has been adapted for use as a games room, and Tim and Ellen can provide you with full details of other activities available nearby, - golf, horse-riding, fishing, and an information folder in each cottage will guide you to the numerous visitor attractions both within Breckland itself, and further afield. *Dolphin Lodge, Roudham Farm, East Harling. Tel: 01953 717126*

Banham   *Map 5 ref H9*
12 miles NE of Thetford, on the B1114

Banham Zoo, about 5 miles to the east of East Harling, provides the opportunity of coming face to face with some of the world's rarest wildlife, - many of the animals who find a home here otherwise facing extinction. The Zoo is particularly concerned with monkeys and apes, but in the 25 acres of landscaped gardens, you'll also come across tigers, cheetahs, lemurs, penguins, and many other species. There are educational talks and displays, a children's play area, Shire Horse dray rides, and a restaurant. The Zoo is open daily all year: more information on 01953 887771.

South Norfolk

This quiet corner of the county is bounded by the Rivers Little Ouse and Waveney which separate Norfolk from Suffolk. The valley of the Waveney is particularly fine and, as one art critic has observed, if the painter John Constable had been born near the northern boundary of Suffolk rather than its southern, he would have found just as much inspiration for his paintings here as he did along the banks of the River Stour. At the time of the Domesday Book, this region was one of the most densely populated in England: today, the small town of Diss is its largest settlement. The physical legacy of those more-populated days is evident in the wealth of Saxon and Norman churches still standing: no fewer than 45 of them with distinctive round towers, exactly 25% of the total number of such structures to be found in the whole of England. We begin our survey at North Lopham and then follow the Waveney eastwards.

North Lopham   *Map 5 ref H10*
7 miles NW of Diss, on the B1113

In the centre of the village is **The King's Head**, a charming old thatched building which dates back to Elizabethan times. The two striking fireplaces in the bars are part of that original structure and the open fires give an extra warmth to the welcome visitors can be assured of receiving here. Your hosts are Ian Thornton, who spent some 24 years in the RAF, and Tim White who has lived in the village all his life and at one time worked as a barman in this very pub. The King's Head has two bars and a separate restaurant which serves excellent traditional English food. The menu, using only fresh produce wherever possible, includes old favourites such as Yorkshire Puddings and Cumberland Sausage, but you'll also find Chilli

The King's Head

con Carne, Spanish Chicken, and a choice of pies and pasties served in a variety of styles. In good weather, you can enjoy your food in the large, lawned garden to the rear of the pub. This is a very appealing place and very convenient if you are visiting nearby Banham Zoo, or going to Bressingham Steam Museum, perhaps for a nostalgic ride on one its vintage locomotives. And naturalists will know the area called Lopham Fen which is one the very few habitats in Britain of the rare Great Raft Spider! *The King's Head, The Street, North Lopham, Norfolk IP22 2NE Tel:01379 687582*

About 4 miles east of North Lopham, off the A1066, is the **Bressingham Steam Museum** which boasts one of the world's finest collections of British and Continental locomotives, amongst them the famous "Royal Scot". A number of the locomotives on display here are on loan from the National Railway Museum at York. All are housed under cover in the museum's extensive locomotive sheds

Bressingham Steam Museum

which also contain many steam-driven industrial engines, traction engines, and *The Fire Museum* whose collection of fire engines and fire-fighting equipment could form a complete museum in its own right. Visitors can view the interior of the Royal Coach and ride along five miles of track through the woods and gardens. The 6 acres of landscaped grounds are notable in themselves since they are planted with more than 5000 Alpine and other types of plant. A 2-acre Plant Centre adjoins the gardens and here there are thousands of plant specimens, many of them rare, available for purchase. Bressingham is renowned for its special "Steam Days'" when the engines can be seen in full steam on the three narrow gauge lines, and talks and footplate rides are given on the standard gauge loco-motives. For further details, ring 01379 687386.

Diss
Map 5 ref I10

19 miles E of Thetford, on the A1066/A140

The late Poet Laureate, John Betjeman, voted Diss his favourite Norfolk town, and it's easy to understand his enthusiasm. The River Waveney running alongside forms the boundary between Norfolk and Suffolk, but this attractive old market town keeps itself firmly on the northern bank of the river. The town is a pleasing mixture of Tudor, Georgian and Victorian houses grouped around *The Mere* which gives the town its name, derived from the Anglo-Saxon word for "standing water".

The old town grew up on the hill above The Mere perhaps be-cause, as an 18th century resident observed, *"all the filth of the town centering in the Mere, beside the many conveniences that are placed over it, make the water very bad and altogether useless;...it stinks exceedingly, and sometimes the fish rise in great numbers, so thick that they are easily taken; they are chiefly roach and eels".* A proper sewerage system was finally installed in 1851.

There's a public park beside the 6-acre Mere and from it a nar-row street leads to the small *Market Place*. This former poultry market is dominated by the somewhat over-restored *St Mary's Church*. The oldest parts date back some 700 years and the St Nicholas Chapel is particularly enjoyable with its wonderful cor-bels, angels in the roof, and gargoyles. In the early 1500s, the Rector here was John Skelton, Court poet and tutor to Prince Henry, later Henry VIII. A bitter, quarrelsome man, Skelton was appointed Poet Laureate through the patronage of Cardinal Wolsey despite the fact that most of Skelton's output has been described as "breathless dog-gerel". Appointed Rector of Diss in 1502, he appears to have been suspended nine years later for having a concubine. Not far from his church is the delightful Victorian Shambles with a cast-iron veranda and a small Museum inside.

Scole
Map 5 ref I10

2 miles E of Diss, on the A140

Scole's history goes back to Roman times since it grew up alongside the Imperial highway from Ipswich to Norwich at the point where it bridged the River Waveney. Traffic on this road (the A140) became unbearable in the 1980s, but a bypass has now mercifully restored some peace to the village. There are two hostelries of note: a coaching inn of 1655, built in an extravagant style of Dutch gables, giant pilasters and towering chimney stacks, and the ***Crossways Inn*** which must have a good claim to being the prettiest pub in the county. Tall and narrow, its half-timbered walls are painted in traditional black and white, and set off by multi-coloured hanging baskets. This lovely old building dates back to around 1570 and its great age is reflected in the antique wood floors, exposed beams and four cavernous open fireplaces. Still more ancient timbers can be seen in the plank doors and around the bar.

The inn's young owners, Leslie and Hugh Edwards, took over here in 1994 and Leslie's menu of wholesome, tasty meals and bar snacks has attracted a loyal clientele. There's a good choice of main meals and amongst the bar snacks the sumptuously filled baguettes are especially popular. Special menus cater for Senior Citizens and children. Outside, two patios covered in grape vines and trailing plants are the place to relax on sunny days and balmy summer eve-

Crossways Inn

nings, surrounded by extensive lawned grounds. In winter time, whole pigs are spit-roasted in the main bar fireplace. Located on the Norfolk-Suffolk boundary, the Crossways Inn is ideal as a base for touring and can offer 3 double-rooms, all en suite, and 1 single with shower. All the rooms are full of character, attractively furnished and equipped with all modern amenities. *Crossways Inn, Bridge Road, Scole, nr Diss, IP21 4DP. Tel: 01379 740638*

Langmere   *Map 5 ref I10*
6 miles NE of Diss, on minor road off the A140, (through Dickleburgh)

In this tiny hamlet, tucked away deep in the countryside near the Suffolk border, visitors to Jill Potterton's **Blacksmith's Cottage & Nursery** can enjoy both a peaceful stay in a charming old cottage and also catch up on their gardening requirements at the adjacent Nursery which specialises in hardy geraniums and cottage garden perennials. Blacksmith's Cottage dates back to the 1830s when it was built for the village wheelwright. It became a private residence many years ago and now provides accommodation with a really cottagey character. Furnished in traditional style, the cottage has

Blacksmith's Cottage and Nursery

just 2 letting rooms. Breakfast, with eggs from Jill's free range hens, is included in the tariff, and evening meals are available by arrangement. Hens aren't the only creatures that Jill keeps on the 4-acre site of the Nursery. As well as ducks, geese, and doves, there are ornamental water-fowl and a rare breed of sheep, the Somali Black Head. And you may well catch sight of those miniature and delightful deer, muntjacs, running wild in the surrounding countryside. *Blacksmith's Cottage & Nursery, Langmere Road, Langmere, nr Dickleburgh, IP21 4QA. Tel: 01379 740982*

Veterans of World War II will be interested in the ***100th Bomb Group Memorial Museum***, a small museum on the edge of Dickleburgh Airfield, (now disused). The Museum is a tribute to the U.S. 8th Air Force which was stationed here during the war, and includes displays of USAAF decorations and uniforms, equipment, combat records and other memorabilia. Facilities include refreshments, a museum shop, visitor centre and a picnic area. The museum is open weekends and Bank Holidays, or by appointment, and admission is free. Tel: 01379 740708.

Harleston
Map 5 ref J9

7 miles NE of Diss, off the A143

This pretty market town with some notable half-timbered and Georgian houses, and a splendid 12th century coaching inn, was a favourite of the renowned architectural authority, Nikolaus Pevsner, who particularly admired the early Georgian Candlers House at the northern end of the town. Another writer has described the area around the market place as *"the finest street scene in East Anglia"*. The town lies in the heart of the Waveney Valley, a lovely area which inspired many paintings by the locally-born artist, Sir Alfred Munnings.

Wortwell
Map 5 ref J9

11 miles NE of Diss, on minor road off the A143

Located in exceptionally beautiful surroundings, the ***Little Lakeland Caravan Park*** is a family-run park on the very edge of the Suffolk border. The 4-acre site, set beside a half-acre lake, has been carefully landscaped to give each caravan an individual pitch

Little Lakeland Caravan Park

of generous proportions, on well-cut grass and usually surrounded by hedging. Jean and Peter Leatherbarrow, who own and run Little Lakeland, are determined not to over-crowd this popular and attractive site, limiting the number of pitches for touring caravans to forty. Booking therefore is strongly recommended, especially during public and school holidays. Jean and Peter also have a small number of modern luxury holiday caravans which may be hired by the week. Each caravan is fully equipped and personally cleaned and inspected before each new letting.

Little Lakeland, which features in Camping & Caravanning's list of Britain's Best Sites, offers its visitors a wide range of amenities. There are modern toilets and showers, electric hook-ups, laundry facilities, a private fishing lake, a children's play area and a quiet area. The site shop sells fresh dairy produce and some basic requirements, including Calor Gas, and there's a Post Office store just a short walk away in the village. The reception at Little Lakeland is well-stocked with information on local attractions and places of interest, - amongst them the Norfolk & Suffolk Aviation Museum at nearby Flixton, and the Otter Trust Centre in the neighbouring village of Earsham. *Little Lakeland Caravan Park, Wortwell, Harleston, IP20 0EL. Tel: 01986 788646*

CHAPTER THREE
King's Lynn and West Norfolk

Sandringham House

Chapter 3 - Area Covered

*For precise location of places please refer to the colour
maps found at the rear of the book.*

3
King's Lynn & West Norfolk

Introduction

It's not at all clear how the huge sea-bite of **The Wash** earned its name: perhaps one should settle for the simple explanation that for centuries it has been trying to wash away as much of the Norfolk and, especially, the Lincolnshire coast as it can. In good weather, The Wash is a placid lake, but when a north, or north-easterly gale blows in, its shallow waters boil up into a spume-flecked, destructive force. It's a mariner's nightmare, feared because of its ever-shifting sandbanks designated by such respectful names as Thief, Bull Dog, Roaring Middle and Pandora. Along most of The Wash's 50-mile shoreline there is no human habitation: in places, the nearest we have ventured is still 5 miles or more from the high-water line. Good news for the more than 160,000 wading birds and 51,000 wild ducks who have claimed the coast for themselves.

It's surprising to find that one of England's most important ports in medieval times, King's Lynn, sat at the southern end of the underwater maze of sandbanks in The Wash. Keels were shallower then, of course, but without such modern aids as echo-sounders it must still have taken sailing skills of a high order to navigate one's way into the safety of King's Lynn harbour.

South of King's Lynn, the countryside never quite decides whether it belongs to the Cambridgeshire fenland with its bread-board level contours and over-arching skyscapes, or to the subtly-rounded undulations of central Norfolk where each twist of the road reveals yet another unblemished rural scene.

King's Lynn   *Map 1 ref C5*

In the opinion of James Lee-Milne, the National Trust's architectural authority, *"The finest old streets anywhere in England"* are to be found at King's Lynn. Tudor, Jacobean and Flemish houses mingle harmoniously with grand medieval churches and stately civic buildings. It's not surprising that BBC Television chose the town to represent early-19th century London in their production of *Martin Chuzzlewit*. It seems, though, that word of this ancient sea-port's many treasures has not yet been widely broadcast, so most visitors to the area tend to stay on the King's Lynn by-pass, making their way to the better-known attractions of the north Norfolk coast. They are missing a lot.

The best place to start an exploration of the town is at the beautiful **Church of St Margaret**, founded in 1101 and with a remarkable leaning arch of that original building still intact. The architecture is impressive but the church is especially famous for its two outstanding 14th century brasses, generally reckoned to be the two largest and most monumental in the kingdom. Richly engraved, one shows workers in a vineyard, the other, commemorating Robert Braunche, represents the great feast which Robert hosted at King's Lynn for Edward III in 1364.

Marks on the tower doorway indicate the church's, and the town's, vulnerability to the waters of the Wash and the River Great Ouse. They show the high-water levels reached during the great floods of 11 March, 1883, (the lowest), then 31 January, 1953, and highest and most recent, a mark dated 11 January, 1978.

The organist at St Margaret's in the mid-18th century was the celebrated writer on music, Dr Charles Burney, but his daughter Fanny was perhaps even more interesting. She wrote a best-selling novel, "Evelina", at the age of 25, became a leading light of London society, a close friend of Dr Johnson and Sir Joshua Reynolds, and at the age of 59 underwent an operation for breast cancer without anaesthetic. She only fainted once during the 20 minute operation and went on to continue her active social life until her death at the age of 87.

Alongside the north wall of St Margaret's is the **Saturday Market Place**, one of the town's two market places, and a few steps further is one of the most striking sights in the town, the **Guildhall of the Holy Trinity** with a distinctive chequerboard design of black flint and white stone. The Guildhall was built in 1421, extended in Elizabethan times, and its Great Hall is still used today for wedding ceremonies and various civic events.

Next door to the Guildhall is the Town Hall of 1895, which in a good-neighbourly way is constructed in the same flint and stone pattern. The Town Hall also houses the **Museum of Lynn Life** where along with displays telling the story of the town's 900 years you can also admire the municipal regalia. The greatest treasure in this collection is King John's Cup, a dazzling piece of medieval workmanship with coloured enamel scenes set in gold. The Cup was supposed to be part of King John's treasure which had been lost in 1215 when his overburdened baggage train was crossing the Nene Estuary and sank into the treacherous quicksands. This venerable legend is sadly undermined by the fact that the Cup was not made until 1340, more than a century after John was dead.

Custom House

A short distance from the Town Hall, standing proudly by itself on the banks of the River Purfleet, is the handsome **Custom House** of 1683, designed by the celebrated local architect, Henry Bell. There's not enough space here to list all of the town's many other important buildings, but mention must be made of the **Hanseatic Warehouse** (1428), the **South Gate** (1440), the **Greenland Fishery Building** (1605), and the **Guildhall of St George**, built around 1406 and reputedly the oldest civic hall in England. The Hall was from time to time also used a theatre and it's known that Shakespeare's travelling company played here. It's considered highly likely that the Bard himself trod the boards. If true, his appearance would be very appropriate since the Guildhall is now home to the **King's Lynn Arts Centre** which is active all year round with events and exhibitions, and since 1951 has arranged an annual Arts Festival in July with concerts, theatre, and a composer in residence. Some of the concerts are held in **St Nicholas' Chapel**, a medieval building whose acoustics outmatch many a contemporary high-tech Concert Hall.

And for an insight into the life of King's Lynn's old fishing community, a visit to **True's Yard** is highly recommended. Two tiny cottages are all that is left of the North End which was once a busy little place with its own boatbuilders, chandlers, sailmakers, pubs, bakehouses and school. Everything else was swept away during the slum clearances of the 1930s. One of the cottages is furnished in the style of the 1850s, the other in that of the 1920s, and they are both stocked with a wealth of memorabilia from the days of fishing under sail, - the tools of the trade, knotwork ornaments, models of the old fishing smacks, vintage photographs and hand-knitted "ganseys".

Tilney St Lawrence
Map 1 ref B6

6 miles SW of Kings Lynn, off the A47

Connoisseurs of ghosts should certainly pay a visit to the **Coach & Horses Inn** since it boasts not just one, but two resident spirits. Both are ladies, and both are very well-behaved. One sits and knits, the other just sits. Anne Howard and Kim Brooke, who run this charming old hostelry, are quite at ease having these supernatural guests sharing their 16th century coaching inn. They seem to fit in,

Coach and Horses Inn

along with the old beams, settle benches (one of them with a 'Penny Throwing Box' beneath it), brasses and porcelain, and a log fire whose chimney has a ladder fixed inside it. The house is listed, the bar too, so even if they wanted to, the owners would not be allowed to remove it. A major attraction at the Coach & Horses is its extensive menu of simple, quality food, carefully prepared and attractively presented. The snack menu includes jacket potatoes, salads, ploughmans and sandwiches, while the main menu offers a good range of fish, meat, and poultry dishes. In addition, the blackboard lists vegetarian options and daily specials, children have their own choices and the dessert menu is also supplemented by daily specials.

On Sundays the Coach & Horses serves a delicious roast lunch from noon until 3.00pm. (booking advisable). The restaurant is non-smoking with a separate area for the addicted, and children are allowed to sit throughout the inn. Outside the white-painted, red-tiled inn, there's a peaceful Beer Garden overlooking open countryside, and a spacious car park. The Coach & Horses is also registered for camping and caravanning, and its convenient location makes this an ideal place to stay, with the many attractions of north-west Norfolk and north Cambridgeshire all within easy reach. *The Coach & Horses Inn, Lynn Road, Tilney St Lawrence, Kings Lynn, PE34 4RU. Tel: 01945 880266*

About 4 miles north of Tilney St Lawrence is Terrington St Clement, a sizeable village notable for the ***"Cathedral of the Marshland"***, a 14th century Gothic masterwork more properly known as St Clement's Church, and for the ***African Violet Centre*** where some quarter of a million violets are grown each year, in a wide range of colour and species.

Downham Market   *Map 1 ref C7*
10 miles S of King's Lynn, off the A10/A1122

Once the site for a major horse fair, this compact little market town stands at the very edge of the Fens, with the River Great Ouse and the New Bedford Drain running side by side at its western edge. Many of its houses are built in the distinctive brick and carrstone style of the area. One of the finest examples of this traditional use of local materials can be seen at Dial House in Railway Road, (now a guest house), which was built in the late 1600s.

The parish church has managed to find a small hill on which to perch. It's an unassuming building with a rather incongruously splendid glass chandelier from the 1730s. Another feature of the town, much loved by postcard manufacturers, is the elegant, riotously decorated cast-iron **Clock Tower** in the market place. This was erected in 1878 at a cost of £450 and "was worth every penny of it!" The tower's backdrop of attractive cottages provides a charming setting for a holiday snap.

Two great names are associated with this small town: Charles I, disguised as a clergyman, stayed at Downham Market for a night during his flight after the Battle of Naseby, and Horatio (later Lord) Nelson, son of the parson of Burnham Thorpe, was sent to the little school here.

It's well worth making the short excursion a couple of miles or so north of Downham Market to **Holy Trinity Church** at Stow Bardolph to see one of the oddest memorials in the country. Before her death in 1744, Sarah Hare, youngest daughter of the Lord of the Manor, Sir Thomas Hare, arranged for a life-sized effigy of herself to be made in wax. It was said to be an exceptionally good likeness: if so, Sarah appears to have been a rather uncomely maiden, and afflicted with boils to boot. Her death was attributed to blood poisoning after she had pricked her finger with a needle, an act of Divine retribution apparently for her sin of sewing on a Sunday. Sarah was attired in a dress she had chosen herself, placed in a windowed mahogany cabinet, and the monument set up in the Hare family's chapel, a grandiose structure which is larger than the chancel of the church itself.

To the southwest of Downham Market, **Denver Sluice** was originally built in 1651 by the Dutch engineer, Cornelius Vermuyden, as part of a scheme to drain 20,000 acres of land owned by the Duke of Bedford. Various modifications were made to the system over the years, but the principle remains the same, and the oldest surviving sluice, built in 1834, is still in use today. Running parallel with it, is the modern **Great Denver Sluice**, opened in 1964: together these two sluices control the flow of a large complex of rivers and drainage channels, and are able to divert floodwaters into the Flood Relief Channel that runs alongside the Great Ouse. The two great drainage cuts constructed by Vermuyden are known as the Old and New Bedford rivers, and the strip of land between them, never more than 1000yds wide, is called the Ouse Washes. This is deliberately allowed to flood during the winter months so that the fields on either side remain dry. The drains run side by side for more than 13 miles, to Earith in Cambridgeshire, and this has become a favourite route for walkers, with a rich variety of bird, animal and insect life to be seen along the way.

Oxborough   *Map 1 ref D7*
10 miles SE of Downham Market, on minor road off the A134

How many hamlets in the country, one wonders, can boast three
such different buildings of note as those to be seen at Oxborough.
Firstly, there's the **Church of St John the Evangelist**, remarkable for its rare brass eagle lectern of 1498, and its glorious
Bedingfeld Chapel of 1525, sheltering twin monuments to Sir
Edmund Bedingfeld and his wife fashioned in the then newly popular material of terracotta.

It was Sir Edmund who built **Oxburgh Hall** (National Trust), a
breathtakingly lovely moated house built of pale-rose brick and white
stone. Sir Edmund's descendants still live in what a later architect,
Pugin, described as *"one of the noblest specimens of domestic architecture of the 15th century"*. Henry VII and his Queen, Elizabeth of
York, visited in 1497 and lodged in the splendid State Apartments
which form a bridge between the lofty gatehouse towers, and which
ever since have been known as the King's Room and the Queen's

Oxburgh Hall

Room. On display here is the original Charter of 1482, affixed with
Edward IV's Great Seal of England, granting Sir Edmund permission to build with "stone, lime and sand", and to fortify the building
with battlements. These rooms also house some magnificent period
furniture, a collection of royal letters to the Bedingfelds, and the
huge Sheldon Tapestry Map of 1647 showing Oxfordshire and Berk-
shire. Another, more poignant, tapestry, known as the Marian
Needlework, was the joint handiwork of Elizabeth, Countess of

Shrewsbury, and Mary, Queen of Scots, during the latter's captivity here in 1570. The Bedingfelds seemed always to draw the short straw when the Tudors needed someone to discharge an unpleasant or difficult task. It was an earlier Sir Edmund who was charged with the care of Henry VIII's discarded wife, Catherine of Aragon, and *his* son, Sir Henry, was given the even more onerous task of looking after the King's official bastard, the Princess Elizabeth. After Elizabeth's accession as Queen, Sir Henry presented himself at Court, no doubt with some misgivings. Elizabeth received him civilly but, as he was leaving, tartly observed that *"if we have any prisoner whom we would have hardlie and strictly kept, we will send him to you"*.

As staunch Catholics, the Bedingfelds were, for the next two and a half centuries, consigned to the margins of English political life. Their estates dwindled as portions were sold to meet the punitive taxes imposed on adherents of the Old Faith. By the middle of the 20th century, the Bedingfelds long tenure of Oxburgh was drawing to a close. In 1951, the 9th Baronet, another Sir Edmund, sold Oxburgh to a builder who promptly announced his intention of demolishing the house. Sir Edmund's mother, the Dowager Lady Sybil, was shocked by such vandalism and used her considerable powers of persuasion to raise sufficient funds to buy back the house. She then conveyed it into the safe keeping of the National Trust.

The grounds at Oxburgh provide the perfect foil for the mellow old building, reflected in its broad moat. There's a wonderfully formal, and colourful, French Garden; a walled Kitchen Garden; and woodland walks. The Hall and Gardens are open from late March to early November: for further details, telephone 01366 318258.

Concluding the trio of interesting buildings in this tiny village is **The Bedingfeld Arms**, an attractive white-painted former coaching inn, backed by trees and overlooking the village green. No-one's quite sure how old the house is, but Trevor and Sue Shoat who run this inviting hostelry believe that it's an 18th century enlargement of much earlier cottages. The food here is definitely rather special, served either in the wood-panelled dining-room, or in the main bar. Seafood is a speciality of the house, but there's also a griddle selection, which includes some hearty steak dishes, and an extensive choice of vegetarian offerings, amongst them a famed "Cambridgeshire Pie", - a home-made wheatmeal crust pastry filled with half a dozen different vegetables and cooked in a rich creamy Stilton sauce. The bar meals include Ploughmans Lunches, pizzas, basket meals, and sandwiches, with a special menu for children.

The Bedingfeld Arms

Real Ale lovers will find a regularly changing selection, along with regulars Theakstons and Batesmans. On fairweather days, you can enjoy your refreshments in the large and peaceful garden at the rear of the inn. And if you're nearby on a Sunday or Bank Holiday Monday, do book ahead for the Traditional Roast Lunch, - exceptionally good value! *Bedingfeld Arms, Oxborough, King's Lynn, PE33 9PS. Tel: 01366 328300*

Hilgay   *Map 1 ref C8*
3 miles S of Downham Market, off the A10

When the Domesday Book was written, Hilgay was recorded as one of only two settlements in the Norfolk fens. It was then an island, its few houses planted on a low hill rising from the surrounding marshland. The village is scarcely any larger today, there's not a lot to see, but collectors of unusual gravestones make their way to its churchyard seeking the last resting-place of George William Manby who, during the Napoleonic wars, invented the rocket-powered life line fired to ships in distress. His gravestone is carved with a ship, an anchor, a depiction of his rocket device, and an inscription that ends with the reproachful words, *"The public should have paid this tribute"*.

Occupying a lovely position near the bridge over the River Wissey at Hilgay, the ***Rose & Crown*** is popular with both road travellers and boating holidaymakers. Bob and Janice Coia and their son Vin-

The Rose & Crown

cent have been here since 1995 and have made this traditional village pub, offering modern entertainments and amenities, an ideal rendezvous at both lunchtime and in the evening. The building itself dates back to the early 1800s but the interior has been lavishly refurbished with high quality furniture and fittings. Colourful tartan tablecloths suggest a Scottish theme and the Coias have added a multitude of attractive and interesting items such as the array of delightful miniatures around the walls, the plaster figurines and a collection of vintage posters and photographs. Other appealing features are the dried flowers on each table and the coloured light windows created by a local craftsman.

The food on offer at the Rose & Crown is equally appealing. Bob is in charge of the kitchen and his specialities include Lamb Madagascar (minced lamb steak, stuffed with garlic and cheese butter, in a creamy green peppercorn sauce) and Chicken Monte Cristo (chicken breast filled with ham, spinach and cheese, in a spicy Provençal sauce). The extensive menu also includes an excellent choice of steak, fish, rice and vegetarian dishes as well as a special selection for children. After a meal here, you may well feel like staying longer. If so, the Rose & Crown has 5 guest rooms (2 double, 2 twin, 1 family) with shared bathroom, shower and WC. They make an ideal base for fishermen, bird watchers, and those wishing to explore the East Anglian countryside. The exquisite Tudor mansion of Oxburgh Hall lies just a few miles to the west, and the incomparable splendours of Ely Cathedral just a little further to the south.

Rose & Crown, Bridge Street, Hilgay, Downham Market, PE38 0LJ. Tel: 01366 385414

Brandon Creek
7 miles S of Downham Market, off the A10

Map 1 ref C9

Where the Little Ouse joins the River Great Ouse stands the historic **Ship at Brandon Creek**. For centuries travellers, journeying by road or water have been stopping off here for refreshment. There are moorings for waterborne travellers and a large car park for those who come by road. The inn was originally built in the 1640s as a dormitory for the labourers working on the Duke of Bedford's massive scheme to drain 20,000 acres of the fens. Today, The Ship enjoys an idyllic riverside setting but back then this was wild country and Fenland people a law unto themselves. One grim tale tells of a landlord of The Ship returning to find that his wife and daughter had been attacked by drunken soldiers. The innkeeper and his friends managed to catch the perpetrators, and buried them up to their necks in the river bank, leaving them to drown as the tide came in. Later, the landlord was consumed by remorse for his violent action and, so it's said, his ghostly figure is often seen walking, hunched in grief, along the riverbank. Stories like this must have fascinated the American novelist and humourist Mark Twain who stayed at The Ship in the 1880s, fell ill here and was nursed back to health.

The present landlords, Tony and Sarah Hook, are untroubled by their ghostly predecessor, and their cheerful and inviting hostelry with its open fires, old beams and brasses soon raises spirits of a

The Ship at Brandon Creek

different kind. Tony is the chef and offers a very extensive choice of steak, fish, poultry and vegetarian meals, and an excellent choice of desserts. Bar Snacks are available at lunchtime, there's a Carvery on Friday and Saturday evenings, and a traditional roast lunch on Sundays. Children are welcome in the dining room and the Forge Bar, so named because at one time the landlord here was also a blacksmith, a combination of trades which was then quite common in rural areas. *The Ship at Brandon Creek, nr Downham Market, PE38 0PP. Tel: 01353 676228*

North of King's Lynn

Roydon *Map 1 ref D4*
6 miles NE of Kings Lynn, off the A148

The sizeable village of Roydon lies on the edge of Roydon Common, at a point where the western heathlands give way to open fields. On the outskirts of this picturesque village is **The Three Horseshoes**, a hostelry with a history going back to the 16th century when it was a coaching inn. Outside, wisteria drapes itself over the warm old brick walls; inside, ancient beams in the low-ceilinged rooms recall those far-off days.

The Three Horseshoes is a typical old country pub with a very friendly atmosphere for which credit must go to the owners, Paul and Maroline Overson, who give a warm welcome to all who visit. The extensive menu of home cooked food on offer can be enjoyed in either the bar, the snug, the restaurant or, in good weather, on the patio. Bar Snacks include basket meals, ploughmans, jacket pota-

The Three Horseshoes

toes and freshly-made sandwiches. The inn is well known for its good family fare and visitors have an excellent choice of meat, fish, and vegetarian dishes, with an additional house special available every day. Children have their own menu and the dessert list always includes a daily choice of gâteau, cheesecake and hot pudding.

The Three Horseshoes is also highly regarded by devotees of real ale, who are treated to a reserve of several real ales on tap. Restaurant and bar meals are available seven days a week and you can book ahead, - particularly advisable if you want to sample the excellent traditional Sunday roast lunch. Hidden away in the heart of the Norfolk countryside, this is definitely a hostelry to seek out. Secluded though it is, the inn is located just four miles from the royal estate of Sandringham, with the lovely north Norfolk coast (a bird-watchers paradise), a host of attractive market towns and villages, and great houses such as Houghton Hall and Holkham Hall, all within easy reach. *The Three Horseshoes, 148, Lynn Road, Roydon, Kings Lynn, PE32 1AQ. Tel: 01485 600362*

Around the corner from The Three Horseshoes, off Broadgate Lane, is **Broadgate Cottage**, a charming property built of local carrstone in the traditional manner and dating back to around 1750. A wonderfully peaceful place for a holiday or a short break, this self-catering cottage shares a mature secluded garden with the friendly owners, Peter and Pauline Rigby, who live next door. Attractively

Broadgate Cottage

furnished, Broadgate Cottage enjoys lovely views either onto the garden or across the surrounding countryside.

There are two bed-rooms, (one double, one twin), each with its own separate staircase. Amenities include a well-equipped kitchen with immersion heater and night storage heater; a sitting room with colour TV, comfortable chairs and an open fire; a separate dining room with pine furniture and another open fire; and a shower-room with electric shower, wash-hand basin and W.C. Outside, as well as the superb garden with its ornamental pond, there is a patio and parking area. And of course, if you get tired of cooking for yourself, The Three Horseshoes inn is just a few steps away.

If you enjoy outdoor pursuits, facilities for fishing, golf and bird-watching are all available locally, and walkers will find a huge choice of footpaths, including walks around the Nature Reserve of Roydon Common. Also nearby, for dedicated walkers, is the Peddar's Way, the old Roman road which leads (eventually) to the Norfolk Coast Path. *Further details from Mr & Mrs P. Rigby, 146, Lynn Road, Roydon, Kings Lynn, PE32 1AQ. Tel: 01485 600424*

Congham
Map 1 ref D4

5 miles NE of Kings Lynn, off the A148

Enjoying a rural and peaceful situation in the village is **The Anvil Inn**, owned and run by Julie and Derek Xice. This listed building, originally 17th century, has been attractively modernised, but the decorative open fireplace in the L-shaped bar room has been retained and, along with stools and copper-topped tables, adds a pleasantly antique flavour to the interior.

The Anvil Inn

Outside, there's an inviting Beer Garden where you'll often see partridges strutting their stuff around the lawn. Popular with bird watchers, walkers, and, during the season, shooting parties, The Anvil offers visitors an excellent choice of traditional English food, served either in the restaurant or in the comfortable bar. Food is available throughout the day and families are welcome.

Congham village lies on the edge of the Bellingham Estate and the Royal Estate of Sandringham lies just five miles away to the north. Houghton Hall, the Marquess of Cholmondeley's magnificent Palladian mansion is just a few miles further to the north-east. *The Anvil Inn, St Andrew's Lane, Congham, Kings Lynn, PE32 1DU. Tel: 01485 600625*

Castle Rising
Map 1 ref C4

5 miles NE of King's Lynn, on minor road off the A148, or A149

As the bells ring for Sunday morning service at Castle Rising, a group of elderly ladies leave the mellow red brick Bede House and walk in procession to the church. They are all dressed in long scarlet cloaks, emblazoned on the left breast with a badge of the Howard family arms. Once a year, on Founder's Day, they add to their regular Sunday costume a tall-crowned hat typical of the Jacobean period, just like those worn in stereotypical pictures of broomstick-flying witches.

These ladies are the residents of the almshouses founded by Henry Howard, Earl of Northampton, in 1614, and their regular Sunday attendance at church was one of the conditions he imposed on the 11 needy spinsters who were to enjoy his beneficence. Howard also required that each inmate of his *"Hospital of the Holy and Undivided Trinity"* must also *"be able to read, if such a one may be had, single, 56 at least, no common beggar, harlot, scold, drunkard, haunter of taverns, inns or alehouses"*.

The weekly tableau vivant of the procession of these blameless virgins to the church seems completely in keeping with this picturesque village which rates high on any "must-not-miss" list of places to visit in Norfolk. The church to which the ladies are making their way, St Lawrence's, although much of it has been reconstructed, is an outstanding example of Norman and Early English work. But overshadowing everything else in this pretty village is the massive **Castle Keep** (English Heritage), its well-preserved walls rising 50ft high, and pierced by a single entrance. The Keep's towering presence is made even more formidable by the huge earthworks on which it stands. The Castle was built in 1150, guarding what was then the sea approach to the River Ouse. (The marshy shore is now some 3 miles distant and still retreating).

Despite its fortress-like appearance, Castle Rising was much more of a residential building than a defensive one. In 1331, when Edward III found it necessary to banish his ferocious French-born mother, Isabella, to some reasonably comfortable place of safety, he chose this far-from-London castle. She was to spend some 27 years here before her death in 1358, never seeing her son again during that time. How could Edward treat his own mother in such a way? Her

Castle Rising

crime, in his view, was that the "'he-Wolf of France", as all her enemies and many of her friends called Isabella, had joined forces with her lover Mortimer against her homosexual husband Edward II, (young Edward's father), and later colluded in the king's grisly murder at Berkeley Castle. A red-hot poker, inserted anally, was the instrument of his death. For three years after that loathsome assassination, Isabella and Mortimer ruled England as Regents. The moment Edward III achieved his majority, he had Mortimer hung, drawn and quartered. His mother he despatched to a lonely retirement at Castle Rising.

Six and a half centuries later, the spacious grounds around the castle provide an appropriate backdrop for an annual display by members of the White Society. Caparisoned in colourful medieval garments and armed with more-or-less authentic replicas of swords and halberds, these modern White Knights stage a battle for control of the castle.

A couple of miles north of Castle Rising is the entrance to **Sandringham Country Park** and **Sandringham House**, the royal family's country retreat where, since 1989, the Queen has chosen to spend every Christmas. Unlike the State Rooms at Windsor Castle and Buckingham Palace where visitors marvel at the awesome trappings of majesty, at Sandringham they savour the atmosphere of a family home. The rooms the visitor sees at Sandringham are those used by the Royal Family when in residence, complete with family portraits and photographs, and comfy armchairs. Successive royal owners have furnished the house with an intriguing medley of the grand, the domestic, and the unusual. Entering the principal reception room, The Saloon, for example, you pass a weighing-machine with a leather-covered seat, a common amenity apparently in great houses of the 19th century. In the same room, with its attractively carved Minstrels' Gallery, hangs a fine family portrait by one of Queen Victoria's favourite artists, Heinrich von Angeli. It shows the Prince of Wales (later Edward VII), his wife Alexandra and two of their children, with Sandringham in the background.

The Prince first saw Sandringham on 4th February 1862. At Victoria's instigation, the 20-year-old heir to the throne had been searching for some time for a country property, a refuge of the kind his parents already enjoyed at Balmoral and Osborne. A courtier accompanying the Prince reported back that although the outside of house was ugly, it was pleasant and convenient within, and set in pretty grounds. The surrounding countryside was plain, he went on, but the property was in excellent order and the opportunity of securing it should not be missed. Within days, the purchase was completed.

Sandringham House

Most of the "ugly" house disappeared a few years later when the Prince rebuilt the main residence; the "pretty grounds" have matured into one of the most beautiful landscaped areas in the country. And the "plain" countryside around, - open heath and grassland overrun by rabbits, has been transformed into a wooded country park, part of the coastal Area of Outstanding Natural Beauty.

One of the additions the Prince made to the house in 1883 was a Ballroom, much to the relief of Princess Alexandra. *"It is beautiful I think & a great success"*, she wrote, *"& avoids pulling the hall to pieces each time there is a ball or anything"*. This attractive room is now used for cinema shows and the estate workers Christmas party. Displayed on the walls is a remarkable collection of Indian weapons, presented to the Prince during his state visit in 1875-6, and hidden away in a recess, are the two flags planted at the South Pole by the Shackleton expedition.

Just across from the house, the old coach-houses and stables have been converted into a fascinating museum. There are some truly splendid royal vehicles here, including the first car bought by a member of the royal family, - a 1900 Daimler, and an evocative series of old photographs depicting the life of the royal family at Sandringham from 1862 until Christmas 1951. Other attractions at Sandringham include a Visitor Centre; Adventure Playground; Nature Walks; Souvenir Shop; Restaurant and Tearoom. For more details, telephone 01553 772675.

Wolferton   *Map 1 ref C3*
8 miles N of King's Lynn, on minor road off the A148
Queen Victoria loved travelling by train. She personally supervised the appointments of the royal coaches that would convey her northwards to her beloved Balmoral, and particularly required that amongst its amenities there should be a bath. Each morning, the royal train would halt in a siding for the royal ablutions to be completed. Her son, later Edward VII, didn't share his mother's enthusiasm for rail travel but it was as a direct response to his purchase of Sandringham House that the Great Eastern railway line was extended to Wolferton, a couple of miles away. Over the main entrance to the station a sign proclaims that *"Through these doors passed all the Kings and Queens of Europe: all others please use the next door"*. From the station's platform, Edward VII waved goodbye to his nephew Kaiser Wilhelm II, (*"Thank God he's gone"* he muttered), and coffins bearing the bodies of George V and George VI began their journey southwards from here, on their way to an Im-

perially ceremonious funeral service that neither of them had wanted. When the line was closed in 1965, British Rail intended to demolish the station, but fortunately one of their own employees, Eric Walker, decided to buy it and save this fascinating piece of royal and railway heritage for the nation. On the day in 1977 that the Queen first opened Sandringham to visitors, Eric opened his **Wolferton Station Museum** where visitors can see the Royal Retiring Rooms, one each for the King and Queen and unchanged since those days, Queen Victoria's travelling bed, and a host of other railway memorabilia. The museum is open daily except Saturdays, April to September: for more details, telephone 01485 540674.

Dersingham
Map 1 ref D3

8 miles N of Kings Lynn, off the A149

This large village just north of Sandringham was actually the source of the latter's name: in the Domesday Book, the manor was inscribed as "Sant-Dersingham": Norfolk tongues found "Sandringham" much easier to get around. Dersingham village has expanded greatly in recent years and modern housing has claimed much of Dersingham Common, although there are still many pleasant walks here through **Dersingham Wood** and the adjoining **Sandringham Country Park**.

An excellent place for bed and breakfast in Dersingham is **The White House** on Hunstanton Road. This substantial Victorian detached house is owned by Valerie Brundle, mother of the well-known motor racing driver, Martin. Valerie herself is an active rally driver

The White House

and scattered around the house are some interesting motor racing memorabilia, including Martin's racing helmet and trophies. Birds are another of Valerie's interests. She is a member of the Royal Society for the Protection of Birds and a keen supporter of the RSPB sanctuary at Snettisham Scalp, just a couple of miles away. The White House has 6 letting rooms, all en suite, and all furnished and equipped to a standard well above their 2 Crowns Commended rating from the ETB. The hearty traditional English breakfast, included in the tariff, will certainly set you up for a day of exploring this appealing corner of the county, whether your preference is for sandy beaches, prime bird-watching areas, or stately homes such as Sandringham House, Holkham Hall and Houghton Hall. *The White House, 44, Hunstanton Road, Dersingham, PE31 6HQ. Tel: 01485 541895/Fax: 544850*

Snettisham
Map 1 ref C3
11 miles N of King's Lynn, off the A149

Snettisham is best known nowadays for its spacious, sandy beaches and the **RSPB Bird Sanctuary**, both about two miles west of the village itself. But for centuries Snettisham was much more famous as a prime quarry for carrstone, an attractive soft-white building-block that provided the "light relief" for the walls of thousands of Georgian houses around the country, and for nearby Sandringham House. The carrstone quarry is still working, its product now destined mainly for "goldfish ponds and the entrance-banks of the more pretentious types of bungalow". Unfortunately, one has to go the British Museum in London to see Snettisham's greatest gift to the national heritage: an opulent collection of gold and silver ornaments from the 1st century AD, the largest hoard of treasure trove ever found in Britain, discovered here in 1991.

In the heart of this delightful village is *The Compasses Inn*, an attractive building of warm old brick with a red-tiled roof. This is very much a family-run pub with Jane and Eddie Sheppard, their son and daughter, all involved in making visitors feel welcome and well looked after. The Compasses is very popular with visitors to the RSPB sanctuary at Snettisham Scalp, and with walkers along the Peddars Way, the long-distance footpath which is a little further away to the east. Recently refurbished to a very high standard, the inn has two bars and two restaurants, one of them non-smoking.

The Sheppards take food seriously and the menu here is quite exceptional. For starters, you could have Crab & Prawn Crepes, followed perhaps by a hearty steak served with a choice of sauces,

The Compasses Inn

or one of the excellent fish dishes. There are also pork, lamb and poultry dishes on offer (half a braised pheasant served in a black cherry sauce, for example), as well as vegetarian options and salads. The regular dessert menu is supplemented by daily Chef's Specials and on no account should you miss out on trying one of them. If you are looking for something light, The Compasses also serves bar snacks at lunchtime.

Outside, there's a secure and secluded Beer Garden, ideal for children, and despite its village centre location the inn also has ample space for parking. If you are thinking of staying in this lovely area, The Compasses has 3 letting rooms, an excellent base from which to explore the north Norfolk coast, the host of charming villages and market towns, the unspoilt countryside and the great houses at Holkham, Houghton and Sandringham. *The Compasses Inn, Lynn Road, Snettisham, King's Lynn, PE31 7PT. Tel: 01485 543270*

Only a quarter of a mile from the beach and the RSPB reserve, **Diglea Caravan & Camping Park** is a quiet, family-run park in a peaceful rural setting. The managers, Chrissie and Steve Chapman, are resident on site, offering their guests a genuinely warm wel-

Diglea Caravan and Camping Park

come and personal attention throughout their stay. Both were formerly in the RAF and Steve is reputed to be an authority on every pub in Norfolk! Their spacious site contains a holiday caravan park and a separate touring and camping field. The amenities are excellent, with full toilet, shower (no charge), laundry and washing-up facilities with razor and hairdryer points also available. There's also a large rally field with toilet/shower block and plenty of electric hook-ups (booking essential at Bank Holidays). Children are well-provided for, with a play area on the touring field and a games room in the clubhouse during opening hours. Dogs with responsible owners are welcome, but must be kept on leads at all times. Diglea also has a small fleet of 2 and 3-bedroomed caravans, all less than 5 years old and fully serviced. With plenty of trees, flowers and ample space between caravans, Diglea provides an excellent setting for a relaxing holiday. *Diglea Caravan & Camping Park, Beach Road, Snettisham, PE31 7RA. Tel: 01485 541367*

On the edge of the village, ***Park Farm*** is a 320-acre working farm which offers visitors a good insight into such farming operations as lambing, shearing, and red deer calving. Children can help feed lambs, kid goats and piglets; take a tractor-drawn safari to see the red deer herd, have a horse or pony ride, try their skills as a potter, or walk a farm trail. There's an Adventure Playground, Craft; Leather and Gift Shops; and a tea room serving home-made refreshments. Open daily throughout the year; for more information call 01485 542425.

About 2 miles north of Snettisham is the famous ***Norfolk Lavender***, the largest lavender-growing and distilling operation in the country. Established in 1932, it is also the oldest. The information point at the western entrance is sited in an attractive listed building which has become something of a Norfolk landmark. On entering the site, visitors instinctively breathe in, savouring the unmistakeable aroma that fills the air. Guided tours of the grounds run throughout the day from the Spring Bank Holiday until the end of September, and during the lavender harvest, visitors can tour the distillery and see how the wonderful fragrance is made.

As well as being a working farm, this is also the home of the National Collection of Lavenders, a living botanical dictionary which displays the many different colours, sizes and smells of this lovely plant. Amongst other attractions at Norfolk Lavender are a Fragrant Meadow Garden, Fragrant Plant Centre, Herb Garden, a Gift Shop selling a wide variety of products, and a tea room serving cream teas and even lavender and lemon scones! Norfolk Lavender is open all year; for further details telephone 01485 570384.

CHAPTER FOUR
The Heartland of Norfolk

Castle Acre

Chapter 4 - Area Covered

*For precise location of places please refer to the colour
maps found at the rear of the book.*

4
The Heartland of Norfolk

Introduction

This central part of the county is effectively a plateau, where the gentle contours never rise or fall more than a few metres. It's far from dull, though. The valleys of the Rivers Nar and Wensum display some of the most enchanting scenery in the county, and the area boasts two of the finest Gothic parish churches in England, at Cawston and Salle.

In pre-historic times, this was the most wooded part of Norfolk, and a good number of medieval natural woods still remain, a feature which adds another visual attraction to this pastoral area of the country. Densely populated during the Middle Ages, the Norfolk heartland today has only two towns of any size, Swaffham and East Dereham, but there is a wealth of quiet, unspoilt villages hidden away on minor roads. We begin our survey at the western end of the region, at the elegant market town of Swaffham

Swaffham   *Map 2 ref E6*
15 miles SE of King's Lynn, on the A47/A1065
Swaffham's one-time claim to be the "Montpellier of England" was justified by the abundance of handsome Georgian houses that used to surround the large, wedge-shaped market place. A good number still survive, along with the **Assembly Room** of 1817 where the quality would foregather for concerts, balls and soirees. The central focus of the market square is the elegant **Butter Cross** presented to the town by the Earl of Orford in 1783. It's not a cross at all but a classical lead-covered dome standing on eight columns and surmounted by a life-size statue of Ceres, the Roman goddess of

Market Cross, Swaffham

agriculture, an appropriate symbol for this busy market town from which ten roads radiate out across the county.

Just off the Market Square, **The Norfolk Hero** makes a pretty picture with its black and white walls and colourful hanging baskets and tubs. The Hero of the name is, of course, the county's most famous son, Horatio Lord Nelson, born in 1758 at Burnham Thorpe

The Norfolk Hero

near the north coast. Although there are some 200 pubs around the country called The Lord Nelson, the owners of the Norfolk Hero, Colin and Margaret Green, believe that theirs is the only one called The Norfolk Hero. There are two separate bars in this welcoming Free House, one with an open wood burning fire, and both decorated with lots of Nelson memorabilia. Bar snacks are available 7 days a week, all home made, and all very competitively priced, as is the excellent Sunday lunch. Local Real Ales are always on tap, along with a Guest Ale, usually IPA; there's a small enclosed beer garden, and on most weekends The Norfolk Hero entertains its guest with live music. *The Norfolk Hero, 48, Station Street, Swaffham, PE37 7HP. Tel: 01760 723923*

From the market place an avenue of limes leads to the quite outstanding **Church of St Peter & St Paul**, a 15th century masterpiece with one of the very best double hammerbeam roofs in the county, strikingly embellished with a host of angels, their wings widespread. The unknown mason who devised the church's harmonious proportions made it 51ft wide, 51ft high and 102ft long. Carved on a bench-end here is a man in medieval dress accompanied by a dog on a chain. The same two figures are incorporated in the town's coat of arms, and also appear in the elegantly designed town sign just beyond the market place. The man is the *"Pedlar of Swaffham"*, a certain John Chapman who according to legend dreamed that if he made his way to London Bridge he would meet a stranger who would make him rich. The pedlar and his dog set off for London and on the bridge he was eventually accosted by a stranger who asked him what he was doing there. John recounted his dream. Scoffingly, the stranger said *"If I were a dreamer, I should go to Swaffham. Recently I dreamt that in Swaffham lived a man named Chapman, and in his garden, buried under a tree, lay a treasure"*. John hastily returned home, uprooted the only tree in his garden, and unearthed two jugs full of gold coins.

There was indeed a John Chapman who contributed generously to the building of the parish church in the late 1400s. Cynics claim however that he was a wealthy merchant, and that similar tales occur in the folk lore of most European countries. Whatever the truth, there's no doubt that the people of Swaffham have taken the story to their hearts.

John Chapman may be Swaffham's best known character locally, but internationally the name of Howard Carter, the discoverer of Tutankhamen's tomb, is much better known. Carter was born at Swaffham in 1874 and his death in 1939 was attributed by the popular press to the "Curse of Tutankhamen". If so, it must have been an extremely sluggish curse. Some 17 years had elapsed since Carter had knelt by a dark, underground opening, swivelled his torch, and found himself the first human being in centuries to gaze on the astonishing treasures buried in the tomb of the teenage Pharaoh.

Move on some 1400 years from the death of Tutankhamen to Norfolk in the 1st century AD. Before a battle, members of the Iceni tribe, led by Boadicea, would squeeze the blue sap of the woad plant onto their faces in the hope of affrighting the Roman invaders, (or any other of their many enemies). At **Cockley Cley Iceni Village and Museums**, 3 miles southwest of Swaffham, archaeologists have reconstructed a village of Boadicea's time, complete with wooden huts, moat, drawbridge and palisades. Reconstruction though it is, the village is remarkably effective in evoking a sense of what daily life for our ancestors entailed more than 1900 years ago.

A recent addition to Swaffham's attractions is the **EcoTech Discovery Centre**, opened in 1998. Through intriguing interactive displays, and hands-on demonstrations, visitors can discover what startling innovations current, and possible, technology may have in store for us during the next millennium.

Castle Acre   *Map 2 ref E5*
4m N of Swaffham, off the A1065

Set on a hill surrounded by water meadows, Castle Acre seems still to linger in the Middle Ages. William de Warenne, William the Conqueror's son-in-law, came here very soon after the Conquest and built a Castle that was one of the first, and largest, in the country to be built by the Normans. Of that vast fortress, little remains apart from the gargantuan earthworks and a squat 13th century, gateway.

Much more has survived of **Castle Acre Priory**, founded in 1090 and set in fields beside the River Nar. Its glorious West Front gives a powerful indication of how majestic a triumph of late Norman architecture the complete Priory must have been. With five apses and twin towers, the ground plan was modelled on the Cluniac mother church in Burgundy where William de Warenne had stayed while making a pilgrimage to Rome. Despite the Priory's great size, it appears that perhaps as few as 25 monks lived here during the Middle Ages. And in some comfort, to judge from the well-preserved Prior's House which has its own bath and built-in wash-basin. The Priory lay on the main route to the famous Shrine at Walsingham with which it tried to compete by offering pilgrims a rival attraction

Castle Acre

in the form of an arm of St Philip. Today the noble ruins of the Priory are powerfully atmospheric, a brooding scene skillfully exploited by Roger Corman when he filmed here for his screen version of Edgar Allan Poe's ghostly story, "The Tomb of Ligeia".

Castle Acre village is extremely picturesque, the first place in Norfolk to be designated a Conservation Area, in 1971. Most of the village, including the 15th century parish church, is built in traditional flint with a few later houses of brick blending in remarkably happily.

Set right in the heart of this lovely village, next to the church, is **Willow Cottage Tea Rooms.** This splendid old cottage, dating back to 1732, is built in the traditional Norfolk materials of red brick and flint and made even more attractive by fragrant climbing roses and tubs of flowers. Inside, old beams and an inglenook fireplace add to the charm. There are soothing views over the village green to one side, open fields to the other. Pamela and Barry Gray own and run these well-known tea rooms where they offer visitors an extensive choice of home-made cakes, scones and pastries, as well as Cream Teas, soup, light lunches and sandwiches. Everything on offer has been cooked on the premises and well-informed visitors make sure they leave space for one of the daily dessert specials, freshly made and served with custard, cream or ice-cream.

If you are exploring Norfolk, this quiet, peaceful village makes an ideal base with the north Norfolk coast, great houses such as Sandringham House and Houghton Hall, and the historic city of

Willow Cottage Tea Rooms

Norwich all within easy reach. Willow Cottage has four guest rooms, (2 double, 2 twin), all pleasingly furnished and decorated. Each room is equipped with television, refreshment tray and complimentary toiletries. *Willow Cottage Tea Rooms, Stocks Green, Castle Acre, PE32 2AE. Tel: 01760 755551*

Commanding one of the best positions in the village, the **Castlegate Restaurant** overlooks the green. It's housed in a building of warm red brick which somehow suggests the warmth of the welcome awaiting you inside. Old beams, sturdy pine furniture, attractive decorative plates, framed water-colours and line drawings all help to create a genuinely welcoming atmosphere. Owners Rex Julian and Alan Howe have been here for more than 12 years now and their reputation for outstanding food is well-established. It could be said that they have their fingers in a lot of pies, as they sell a tempting range of these along with an impressive selection of more elaborate English and continental dishes.

Everything on the menu is home-made and all dishes are prepared using only the freshest local ingredients. There's an excellent choice of starters (from the Chef's special soup of the day through home-made Duck and Liver Pâté to Japanese Prawns), and an equally varied selection of main dishes: steaks, chicken and fish. Castlegate Restaurant is open seven days a week for breakfast, morning coffee, lunch and afternoon tea, with evening meals served

Castlegate Restaurant

from Wednesday to Saturday. Booking is advisable for Sunday lunch as it proves very popular with locals and visitors alike.

Rex and Alan also own the delicatessen and general store next door to the Castlegate Restaurant where you'll find an excellent choice of sweet and savoury delicacies. *Castlegate Restaurant, Stocks Green, Castle Acre, Kings Lynn, P32 2AE. Tel: 01760 755340*

On the outskirts of this attractive village is **Lodge Farm**, a substantial old farmhouse with breathtaking views across the west Norfolk countryside. Here Hugh and Edwina Coghill offer guests excellent bed and breakfast accommodation in a non-smoking environment. The farmhouse stands in 600 acres of land forming part of the Holkham Estate, owned by the Earls of Leicester. (The Earls' magnificent Palladian mansion, Holkham Hall, about 18 miles away, is one of the great sights of Norfolk and should not be missed). Lodge Farm itself stands in large gardens and has three paddocks, usually stocked with sheep and some horses. Extensive lawns, noble trees and a large natural pond favoured by ducks and other wildlife create a marvellously peaceful and soothing atmosphere.

The house was built on a grand scale some 200 years ago in the Georgian style with spacious, gracefully proportioned rooms throughout. There are 3 guest rooms, all twin-bedded. One is en suite, the other two share a bathroom. Like the rest of the house, these rooms are elegantly furnished and well-equipped. Breakfast at Lodge Farm is also something special, with only the very best ingredients used: fresh farm eggs, tasty Castle Acre sausages from the local butcher,

Lodge Farm

and home-made marmalade. Thus fortified, you might feel ready to tackle a stretch of the famous long-distance walk, the Peddars Way, which passes through the village. This 50-mile route stretches from the Suffolk border to the north Norfolk coast, following an original road laid down by the Romans around AD60. Traversing gentle terrain, the Peddars Way for much of its course is a text-book example of a straight-as-an-arrow Roman thoroughfare. A rare exception occurs at Castle Acre where the route deviates in order to negotiate a ford across the River Nar. *Lodge Farm, Castle Acre, King's Lynn, PE32 2BS. Tel: 01760 755506*

Litcham
Map 2 ref F5

11 miles NE of Swaffham, on the B1145

In the very heart of this village strung alongside the infant River Nar is the **Bull Inn**, standing on a site where, in one guise or another, there has been a hostelry since 1460. This wonderful old building has evolved over the years rather than been planned. The interior of this historic structure has been latterly refreshed by an interior designer and the general result is one of cosy intimacy within the environment of an ancient inn. There are two eating areas: the lounge/restaurant, and bar. There's also an attractive courtyard which, when the weather is fine, enables folk to enjoy a beer or two in the former coaching yard.

The Bull is a pub which tries its utmost to cater for all of a discerning nature, and it is "children-friendly". The genial mood is matched by an agreeable and proficiently trained staff who respect old-fashioned service and strive to satisfy their patrons.

The Bull

The food on offer at the Bull Inn is a marvellous alliance of the firm favourites, including vegetarian versions, and the innovative. The Bull's reputation for really excellent food is well-deserved, and booking is recommended. The chef is glad to prepare meals for special diets. The wines are especially pleasing. Directly imported, they represent singularly good value and offer a choice of varieties from all over the world. Three or four Real Ales, and nearly all the leading brand keg and bottled beers, are also available.

Open all day, seven days a week, the Bull Inn is very popular with villagers and visitors alike. This is a marvellous spot to have a meal - whether it's lunch, supper, or a snack at any time. Instead, or as well, one can enjoy a morning coffee, a fine pint, or a glass of wine, in good company and a friendly ambiance. *The Bull Inn, 2 Church Street, Litcham. Tel: 01328 701340*

Small though it is, Litcham can boast an intriguing **Village Museum**, with displays of local artefacts from Roman times to the present, an extensive collection of photographs, some of which date back to 1865, and an underground lime kiln. The museum is open weekend afternoons, or by appointment, and admission is free. Tel: 01328 701383.

East Dereham   Map 2 ref G6
16 miles W of Norwich, on the A47

One of the most ancient towns in the county, East Dereham has a recorded history stretching back to 654AD when St Withburga founded a Nunnery here. Her name lives on at **St Withburga's Well**, just to the west of the church. This is where she was laid to rest but, some 300 years later, the Abbot and monks of Ely robbed her grave and ensconced the precious, fund-raising relic in their own Cathedral. In the saint's desecrated grave a spring suddenly bubbled forth, its waters possessed of miraculous healing properties, and St Withburga's shrine attracted even more pilgrims than before. Some still come.

In the Church of St Nicholas, the second largest in Norfolk, there are features from every century from the 12th to the 16th: a magnificent lantern tower, a lofty Bell Tower, painted roofs, and a Seven Sacrament Font. This is the largest of these notable fonts of which only 30 have survived, 28 of them in Norfolk and Suffolk.

In the northeast transept is buried a poet some of whose lines have become embedded in the language:

> *"Variety's the very spice of life, the monarch of all I survey*
> *God made the country and man made the town".*

They all came from the pen of William Cowper who, despite being the author of such cheery poems as "John Gilpin", suffered grievously from depression, a condition not improved by his association with John Newton, a former slave trader who had repented and become "a man of gloomy piety". The two men collaborated on a book of hymns which included such perennial favourites as *"Oh! for a closer walk with God"*, *"Hark, my soul, it is the Lord"*, and *"God moves in a mysterious way"*. Cowper spent the last four years of his life at East Dereham, veering in and out of madness. In a late-flowering romance, he had married the widow Mary Unwin but the strain of caring for the deranged poet drove her in turn to insanity and death. She too is buried in the church.

William died four years after Mary, in 1800. Three years later another celebrated writer was born at the quaintly named hamlet of **Dumpling Green** on the edge of the town. George Borrow was to become one of the great English travel writers, producing books full of character and colour such as "Wild Wales" and "The Bible in Spain". In his autobiographical novel "Lavengro" he begins with a warm recollection of the town where he was born: *"I love to think on thee, pretty, quiet D[ereham], thou pattern of an English market town,* *with thy clean but narrow streets branching out from thy modest market place, with thine old-fashioned houses, with here and there a roof of venerable thatch"*. The house in which George Borrow was born, Borrow's Hall, still stands in Dumpling Green.

A much less attractive character connected with East Dereham is Bishop Bonner, the enthusiastic arsonist of Protestant "heretics" during the unhappy reign of Mary Tudor. He was rector of the town before being appointed Bishop of London and he lived in the exquisite thatched terrace now called **Bishop Bonner's Cottages**. The exterior is ornamented with delightful pargetting, a frieze of flower and fruit designs below the eaves, a form of decoration which is very unusual in Norfolk. The cottages now house a small Museum.

Three miles northwest of Dereham, off the B1146 road at **Gressenhall**, is the **Norfolk Rural Life Museum**. It's housed in a former workhouse which, like so many of those detested institutions, is an extremely imposing late 18th-century building, this one built in rose-red brick. Gressenhall Workhouse was designed to accommodate some 700 unfortunates, so it was built on a very grand scale indeed. There's ample room for the many exhibits illuminating the working and domestic life of Norfolk people over the last 150 years. The surrounding 50 acres of countryside, Union Farm, is run as a typical 1920s farm, with rare breeds of sheep, pigs, cattle and poultry, and demonstrations of the real nature of bygone agricultural labour. The museum hosts numerous special events during the season, ranging from Steam Days to an international folk dance festival with more than 200 dancers taking part. For more details, telephone 01362 860563.

A mile or so south of Gressenhall, the tiny community of **Dillington** has great difficulty in getting itself noticed on even the most large-scale of maps. This very Hidden Place is worth seeking out for **Norfolk Herbs at Blackberry Farm**, a specialist herb farm located in a beautiful wooded valley. Visitors are invited to browse through a vast collection of aromatic, culinary and medicinal herb plants, and to learn all about growing and using herbs. Admission is free. For more details (and directions) phone 01362 860812.

Brisley   Map 2 ref G4
7 miles N of East Dereham, on the B1145

Set in the heart of the village, **The Brisley Bell** is a beautiful old building dating back to the 16th century. Inside the inn there are beamed ceilings and lots of old timber, and traditional log fires all add to the warmth and friendly atmosphere. The owners of The

The Brisley Bell

Brisley Bell, Jeremy and Lynn, welcome families as they a young daughter of their own. They also delight in owning a wide variety of farm animals including horses, pygmy goats, chickens, guinea pigs, etc, that reside in 6 acres of privately owned ground at the Bell.

The bar menu offers an excellent choice of hot dishes, including traditionally home-made lasagne and the Brisley Bell mixed grill. Cold dishes range from Ploughman's lunch to an excellent selection of sandwiches and baguettes. There is also a superb kid's menu selection. All produce is locally supplied, including the fish fresh from Lowestoft fish markets which is the speciality of the house. This can be enjoyed in the bar, or alternatively in the non-smoking restaurant. Jeremy really excels himself with these fish dishes, alongside a wide selection of steaks and vegetarian options, and if you're still hungry there are plenty of delicious desserts to choose from.

Brisley village itself is well-known to local historians and naturalists for its huge expanse of heathland, some 170 acres of it. It's reckoned to be the best example of unspoilt common in Norfolk and at its centre are scores of pits which were dug out in medieval times to provide clay for the wattle and daub houses of the period. Another feature of interest in the village is Gately Manor (private), an Elizabethan manor house standing within the remains of a medieval moat, and yet another moated house at Old Hall Farm in the south-west corner of the green. *The Brisley Bell, The Green, Brisley, NR20 5DW. Tel: 01362 668686*

A couple of miles east of Brisley, near the village of **North Elmham**, stand the sparse remains of a **Saxon Cathedral**. North

Elmham was the seat of the Bishops of East Anglia until 1071 when they removed to Thetford, and 20 years later to Norwich. Although there had been a cathedral here since the late 7th century, what has survived is mostly from the 11th century. Despite its grand title, the T-shaped ground plan reveals that the cathedral was no larger than a small parish church.

Foxley   *Map 3 ref H4*
15 miles NW of Norwich, off the A1067

This delightful village makes an ideal base for a touring holiday and ***Moor Farm Holidays*** can offer visitors a wide choice of attractive accommodation. Right in the centre of the village and close to the River Wensum (ideal for anglers) is "Heather Cottage", a very bright property with an exceptionally well maintained lawned garden complete with summer house and fish pond. At Moor Farm itself is "Moor Farm Cottage", an appealing period cottage dating back over 300 years and offering very comfortable and spacious accommodation. It too has its own garden. Also on the farm is "The Stables", recently converted to provide outstanding accommodation in a very peaceful location. With the disabled in mind, two of them have been fitted with extra wide doors, shower rooms designed for wheelchair access, and other specialised fittings. There are 8 cottages in all, sleeping from 3 to 6 people. "Heather Cottage" can accommodate four;"Moor Farm Cottage" up to seven. "The Stables" will also be of particular interest to anglers since the owner has fishing rights on the River Wensum. Day ticket fishing is also available further downstream and anglers are also welcome to fish on the farm's own well-stocked pond.

Moor Farm Holidays

Walkers and bird-watchers will find 365 acres of mature Norfolk Naturalist Trust woodland right next door to Moor Farm, and the historic houses of Blickling Hall, Holkham and Sandringham are all within easy reach, as are the Norfolk Broads and the North Norfolk coast. Or you might want to visit the famous Thursford collection, ten miles away, and hear its mighty Wurlitzer organ in operation! *Moor Farm Holidays, Moor Farm, Foxley, Dereham, NR20 4QN. Tel/Fax: 01362 688523*

About 4 miles southeast of Foxley, at **Great Witchingham**, is **Philip Wayre's Norfolk Wildlife Centre & Country Park**, home to an interesting collection of rare, or ancient, breeds of farm livestock such as white-faced woodland and Shetland sheep, pygmy goats and Exmoor ponies. Set in 40 acres of peaceful parkland, the Centre also has reindeer, otters, and badgers, pools teeming with wildfowl and a huge colony of wild herons nesting in the trees. There are also commando and Adventure Play Areas; one of the finest collection of trees and flowering shrubs in the county; a cafe and gift shop.

A little further southeast, the **Dinosaur Adventure Park** near Lenwade doesn't have any living creatures, but as you wander through the woods here you will come across some startlingly convincing life-size models of dinosaurs. One of them, the "Climb-a-Saurus", is a children's activity centre. A woodland maze; a picnic area with gas-fired barbecues; a play area for toddlers; a restaurant, and a Dinostore offering a wide variety of dinosaur models, books and gifts, are amongst the other attractions. Open from early April to late October: for more details, telephone 01603 870245.

Anyone who has ever read Parson Woodforde's enchanting *Diary of a Country Parson* will want to make a short diversion to the tiny village of **Weston Longville**, a mile or so south of the Dinosaur Park. The Revd James Woodforde was vicar of this remote parish from 1774 until his death in 1803, and throughout that time he conscientiously maintained a daily diary detailing a wonderful mixture of the momentous and the trivial. "Very great Rebellion in France" he notes, when 10 days after the Fall of the Bastille, the dramatic news eventually arrived at Weston Longville. More often he is recording his copious meals, ("We had for dinner a Calf's head, boiled Fowl and Tongue, a saddle of Mutton roasted on the side table, and a fine Swan roasted with Currant Jelly Sauce for the first Course. The Second Course a couple of Wild Fowl, Larks, Blamange, Tarts etc. etc."); the weather, (during the winter of 1785, for example, the frost was so severe that it froze the chamberpots under the beds); and his frequent dealings with the smuggler Andrews who kept the good parson well-supplied with contraband tea, gin and cognac. Inside the simple village church there's a portrait of Parson Woodforde, painted by his nephew, and across the road the inn has been named after this beguiling character.

Cawston   *Map 3 ref I4*
12 miles NW of Norwich, on the B1145

"Lovers of the Norfolk churches can never agree which is the best", wrote Sir John Betjeman. *"I have heard it said that you are either a Salle man or a Cawston man"*. In this county so rich in exceptionally beautiful churches, Salle and Cawston are indeed in a class of their own. **St Agnes Church** in Cawston, amongst many other treasures, boasts a magnificent double hammerbeam roof, where angels with protective wings eight feet across float serenely from the roof, and a gorgeous 15th century rood screen embellished with lovely painted panels of saints and Fathers of the Church. The two churches are just a couple of miles apart so you can easily decide for yourself whether you are "a Salle man or a Cawston man". Surprisingly for such a genial character, Sir John seems to have overlooked the possibility that other visitors to these two remarkable churches might define themselves as either "a Salle woman or a Cawston woman".

On the edge of Cawston village is **Broadland Wineries**, a family-owned business which was established in 1965 and moved to its 4.5 acre site here in 1971. Around 100 long-serving local staff are employed here, making the company vital to the economy of this rural community. Broadland Wineries is perhaps best known for its White House English Perry, named after the two 18th century cottages which still stand on the winery site. It sells around 2 million magnums of this refreshing still Perry which has an alcoholic strength of 7.5% by volume. The company also supplies a range of 20 traditional Fruit Wines. These attractive wines are distributed nationwide amongst the independent trade, licensed delicatessens and other specialist outlets.

The statistics of the winery's output are quite staggering: it produces 3.25 million litres of White House Perry, and 3.5 million litres of fortified British wine (formerly known as British sherry, a term which is no longer legal). In addition, Broadland Wineries have become heavily involved in the contract bottling business and are currently bottling wine from Australia, Argentina, Chile, California, Hungary, Romania and South Africa. In 1996, the winery bottled more than 7 million litres from these countries but there is capacity

Broadland Wineries

at the site for more than three times that figure. One more statistic: the winery has storage capacity here for some 4 million litres.

The company also supplies multiple retailers with "own label" wines and through its own in-house designer service has instigated new trends in eye-catchingly different label designs. Broadland Wineries regularly welcomes present and potential contract bottling customers from all over the world to visit its premises to taste existing products or others specially blended to meet their requirements. There is also a small retail shop where members of the public are welcome to buy the range of fruit and country wines. *Broadland Wineries, The New Winery, Chapel Street, Cawston, NR10 4BG. Tel: 01603 872474 Fax: 01603 871312*

For those looking for a rather special location, it's well worth finding the **Haveringland Hall Caravan Park**, just outside Cawston. The site is well-hidden, eight miles north-west of Norwich and a mile west of the B1149 (it may be necessary to phone the park manager for directions). The Caravan Park was established in 1953 in the grounds of Haveringland Hall, now

Haveringland Hall Caravan Park

demolished, but formerly the Residence of Baron de Ramsey.

There is a well-stocked 12 acre lake which can be fished by Caravan Park visitors, many beautiful woodland walks and an arboretum filled with specimen trees. An interesting feature of Haveringland is it's medieval stocks. Haveringland Hall Caravan Park provides the peace and quiet so essential in the rush of modern life and is an ideal base for exploring the beautiful Norfolk countryside and the many nearby places of interest. *Haveringland Hall Caravan Park, Cawston, Norfolk, NR10 4PN Tel/Fax: 01603 871302*

Hevingham   Map 3 ref J5
8 miles N of Norwich, off the A140

Once you've seen it, its walls painted a lovely peachy-cream and decked with colourful hanging-baskets of flowers, it's difficult to drive by without stopping at ***The Fox*** on the A140 between Norwich and Cromer. The pub is run by Pamela and Ian Campbell who, in their early forties, became bored with their current occupations: Pamela was a housewife, Ian a welder. They both fell in love with the idea of managing a pub. As it turned out, they've managed very well because the hostelry they took over in 1997 is now one of the most popular in the area. Some of the appeal lies in the quaint old building, parts of which date back to the 17th century. Even before that, there was an alehouse here which was a favoured refuge for monks

The Fox

from the monastery which then stood just across the road. An old legend claims that there was an underground tunnel linking the monks' austere cells to the much more convivial drinking-place which is now The Fox. The tunnel has yet to be discovered, but there are frequent reports of ghostly monkish figures roaming the premises, apparently in search of a good jug of ale. They will certainly find that here, along with an excellent choice of wholesome, well-prepared food. *The Fox, Cromer Road, Hevingham, NR10 5LY. Tel: 01603 755362*

Aylsham

Map 3 ref J4

14 miles N of Norwich, on the A140

From Hevingham, the A140 leads due north to the attractive little town of Aylsham, set beside the River Bure, the northern terminus of the **Bure Valley Railway**. It has an unspoilt **Market Place**, surrounded by late 17th and early-18th century houses, reflecting the prosperity the town enjoyed in those years from the cloth trade, and a 14th/15th century church, St Michael's, said to have been built by John O'Gaunt. In the churchyard is the tomb of one of the greatest of the 18th century landscape gardeners, Humphrey Repton, the creator of some 200 parks and gardens around the country.

One of Repton's many commissions was to landscape the grounds of **Blickling Hall** (National Trust), a "dream of architectural beauty", which stands a mile or so outside Aylsham. Many visitors have marvelled at their first sight of the great Hall built for Sir Henry Hobart in the 1620s. *"No-one is prepared on coming downhill past the church into the village, to find the main front of this finest of Jacobean mansions, actually looking upon the road, unobstructedly, from behind its velvet lawns"* enthused Charles Harper in 1904. *"No theatrical manager cunning in all the artful accessories of the stage could devise anything more dramatic"*.

From the outside, Sir Henry's house fully satisfied the current architectural vogue for perfect symmetry. Four towers topped with lead-covered turret-caps rise at each corner, there are lines of matching Dutch gables and mullioned windows, and even the chimneys were placed in corresponding groups of twos, threes or fours.

Inside, the most spectacular feature is the Long Gallery which extends for 135ft and originally provided space for indoor exercise in bad weather. Its glory is the plaster ceiling, an intricately patterned expanse of heraldic panels bearing the Hobart arms, along with others displaying bizarre and inscrutable emblems such as a naked lady riding a two-legged dragon.

Other treasures at Blickling include a dramatic double-flight carved oak staircase, the Chinese Bedroom lined with 18th century hand-painted wallpaper, and the dazzling Peter the Great Room. A descendant of Sir Henry Hobart, the 2nd Earl of Buckinghamshire, was appointed Ambassador to Russia in 1746, and he returned from

May Day at Blickling Hall

that posting with a magnificent tapestry, the gift of Empress Catherine the Great. This room was re-designed so as to display the Earl's sumptuous souvenir to its full effect, and portraits of himself and his Countess by Gainsborough were added later.

The Earl was a martyr to gout and his death in 1793 at the age of 50 occurred when, finding the pain unbearable, he thrust his bloated foot into a bucket of icy water, and suffered a heart attack. He was buried beneath the idiosyncratic Egyptian Pyramid in the grounds, a 45ft high structure designed by Ignatius Bonomi who combined Egyptian and classical elements to create a mausoleum which, if nothing else, is certainly distinctive.

Blickling also offers its visitors miles of footpaths through lovely grounds, a Plant Centre, Picnic Area, Restaurant and Shop. Tel: 01263 733084

Within a few miles of Blickling Hall are two other stately homes, both the properties of Lord and Lady Walpole. Neither of the houses, *Mannington Hall* and *Wolterton Park*, is normally open to the public but their gardens and grounds are. At Mannington there are country walks and trails, a Heritage Rose Garden featuring thousands of roses set in small gardens reflecting their period of origin, a Garden Shop, and tea room. Wolterton Park, the stately 18th century Hall built for Horatio Walpole, brother of Sir Robert, England's first Prime Minister stands in grounds landscaped by Humphrey Repton. Here there are miles of waymarked walks and trails, orienteering, an Adventure Playground and various special events are held throughout the year. For more information on either property, call 01263 761214

Just north of Mannington Hall stands the village of **Little Barningham** where St Mary's Church is a magnet for collectors of ecclesiastical curiosities. Inside, perched on the corner of an ancient box pew, stands a remarkable wood-carved skeletal figure of the Grim Reaper. Its fleshless skull stares hollow-eyed at visitors with a defiant, mirthless grin: a scythe gripped in one clutch of bones, and an hour-glass in the other, symbolise the inescapable fate that awaits us all. This gruesomely powerful memento mori was donated to the church in 1640 by one Stephen Crosbie who, for good measure, added the inscription: *"As you are now, even so was I, Remember death for ye must dye"*. Those words were a conventional enough adjuration at that time, but what is one supposed to make of Stephen's postscript inscribed on the back of the pew: *"For couples joined in wedlock this seat I did intend"*?

CHAPTER FIVE
The Northwest Coast

Holkham Hall

Chapter 5 - Area Covered

*For precise location of places please refer to the colour
maps found at the rear of the book.*

5
The Northwest Coast

Introduction

Norfolk has more than a hundred miles of coastline and in this chapter we explore the 17-mile stretch from Hunstanton eastwards. Even in this comparatively short distance the shoreline changes from the perfect sands at Hunstanton to salt marshes threaded by winding creeks, and windswept dunes barely held in place by marram grass. It's an exhilarating coast, with huge skies, ozone-tangy breezes sweeping in from the North Sea, and an abundance of wildlife. There are three separate Nature Reserves within an 8-mile stretch, including the huge National Trust-owned bird sanctuary of Scolt Head Island.

The whole of the North Norfolk coast is of course a twitchers' paradise, with an extraordinary number of different species of birds to be spotted. An admirable way to experience the area to the full is to walk all or part of the Coastal Footpath which begins at Holme next the Sea and follows the coastline for some 36 miles eastwards to Cromer, for most of its route well away from any roads.

Although the whole of Norfolk lies on a foundation of chalk, 1000ft deep in places, it is only in this northwest corner that it lies close enough to the surface to have been used as a building material. Once exposed to the air, the chalk, or "clunch" as it's known, becomes a surprisingly durable material. It was widely used in medieval buildings and can still be found in many barns, farmhouses and cottages in the area. Chalk was also quarried and then burnt to produce lime, prodigious quantities of which were used in building the sublime churches of the Middle Ages.

We begin our journey through this captivating corner of the county at Hunstanton, a busy seaside resort which can boast two unique features: one, it has the only cliffs in England made up of colourful levels of red, white and brown strata, and two, it is the only east coast resort that faces west, looking across The Wash to the Lincolnshire coast and the unmistakeable tower of the 272ft high Boston Stump, (more properly described as the Church of St Botolph).

Hunstanton

Hunstanton town is a comparative newcomer, developed in the 1860s by Mr Hamon L'Estrange of nearby Hunstanton Hall to take advantage of the arrival of the railway here, and to exploit the natural appeal of its broad, sandy beaches. The centre is well-planned with mock-Tudor houses grouped around a green that falls away to the shore. Hunstanton's social standing was assured after the Prince of Wales, later Edward VII, came here to recover from typhoid fever. He stayed at the Sandringham Hotel which, sadly, has since been demolished, along with the grand Victorian pier, and the railway. But Hunston, as locals call the town, still has a distinct 19th century charm about it and plenty to entertain visitors.

The huge stretches of sandy beach, framed by those multi-coloured cliffs, are just heaven for children who will also be fascinated by the **Kingdom of the Sea**, on the South Promenade, where an underwater glass tunnel provides a fascinating opportunity to watch the varied and often weird forms of marine life that inhabit Britain's waters. A popular excursion from Hunstanton is the boat trip to **Seal Island**, a sandbank in The Wash where seals can indeed often be seen sunbathing at low tide.

The Cliffs at Hunstanton

Just a few minutes walk from Hunstanton's glorious sandy beaches and close to the town centre, **The Gables** is a family-run guest house offering visitors a very comfortable and relaxing atmosphere. The spacious Edwardian house, built in traditional Norfolk carrstone, has been totally refurbished and tastefully appointed by Barbara Bamfield and her husband, a builder. The high quality furnishings, the interesting memorabilia and old photographs, give a wonderfully warm and friendly feel to the whole house. All five bedrooms have en suite facilities and are attractively furnished to a very high standard. All are well-equipped and most enjoy a view of the sea. Food is taken seriously at The Gables. A full English or continental breakfast is served in the spacious dining room, and with prior booking special diets, packed lunches, afternoon teas, children's menu and full evening meals, offering a varied selection of dishes made from fresh local produce are also available. Children are welcome, and a travel cot

The Gables

and high chair can be supplied. (Regretfully, pets cannot be accommodated, and smoking is not permitted). Hunstanton is well-known for the range and variety of its holiday attractions, and you only have to travel a little further afield to find many more places of interest: the famous lavender farm at Heacham, for example; glassmaking by Caithness Crystal in the lovely old market town of King's Lynn; the great houses of Sandringham, Holkham and

Houghton; and the birdwatchers' paradise which extends for miles along the coast. *The Gables, 28, Austin Street, Hunstanton, PE36 6AW. Tel: 01485 532514*

Old Hunstanton

Map 2 ref C1

1 mile N of Hunstanton, off the A149

With its mellow old houses and narrow winding lanes, Old Hunstanton is utterly charming. The sand dunes and creeks provide a perfect habitat for interesting varieties of colourful flora, - sea poppies, samphire, marram and sea lavender and more. The glorious sands continue here, and the **Norfolk Coast Path** leads eastwards all the way to Cromer, some 36 miles distant.

Few hotels can have had such a curious past as the **Lakeside Hotel** in Old Hunstanton. It was originally built around 1890 as a waterworks serving this peaceful coastal village, and converted into a hotel almost a century later. Perhaps the most striking feature is the spring-fed lake, once the reservoir, about 150ft square but only 2ft deep. It provides a wonderfully soothing place where guests can relax with a book or just watch the swans, ducks and coots who nest on the lake's two tiny islands. This corner of north-west Norfolk is noted for the abundance and variety of its bird-life so you may well hear night-jars and skylarks as they soar over the nearby Golf Club (which, incidentally, is open to visitors).

The Lakeside Hotel is owned by Liz and Keith Clayson-Hoffbauer, both former teachers, who provide their guests with a warm welcome and personal service to ensure that their stay is as relaxed and comfortable as possible. There are eight letting rooms, six of

The Lakeside Hotel

them double or twin-bedded, and two single rooms. The single rooms share a bathroom whilst the others are all en suite. Liz and Keith are both adept in the kitchen and pride themselves on their home cooking, using fresh produce wherever possible.

Breakfast, served in the elegant conservatory overlooking the lake, is included in the tariff and 3-course evening meals are also available with a vegetarian choice always on the menu. Lakeside is licensed for residents and restaurant guests. Substantial packed lunches are also available and should be ordered the day before. Smokers should note that Lakeside operates a no smoking policy in all rooms except in the comfortable lounge with its sink-into Chesterfield sofas. And if you can tear yourself away from Lakeside, you will find a host of local attractions such as golf, birdwatching, walking, craft centres, stately homes, museums, beaches and much more all within easy reach. *Lakeside Hotel, Waterworks Road, Old Hunstanton, PE36 6JE. Tel: 01485 533763*

Ringstead   Map 2 ref D2
3 miles E of Hunstanton, on minor road off the A149

Another appealing village, with pink and white-washed cottages built in wonderfully decorative Norfolk carrstone. A rare Norman round tower, all that survives of St Peter's Church, stands in the grounds of the former Rectory and adds to the visual charm.

In a region well-provided with excellent nature reserves, the one on **Ringstead Downs** is particularly attractive, and popular with picnickers. The chalky soil of the valley provides a perfect habitat for the plants that thrive here and for the exquisitely marked butterflies they attract.

Located on the outskirts of this unspoilt village and surrounded by beautiful countryside, **Sedgeford Road Farm Holiday Cottages** more than deserve their English Tourist Board rating of 5 Keys, Highly Commended. The Good Holiday Cottage Guide also heaped praise on these two "absolute delights", noting their "beautifully cared for interiors, deep sofas and armchairs, the most appealing pictures and prints we have seen on our travels, attractive lamps, pretty curtains, good fitted carpets, peace and quiet". These two exceptional cottages have been carefully converted from old farm buildings, beautifully furnished and well-equipped with central heating and double glazing. "Tumblers" was formerly the old cart shed which used to house the old Norfolk "Tumbler" carts, hence the name. The 2-bedroomed building has been sympathetically converted with many of the original features, such as the

Sedgeford Road Farm Holiday Cottages

exposed beams, still in place. The other cottage, "Pickles Patch", (named after owner Margaret Greer's beloved cat), has 3 bedrooms, its own partly-enclosed patio, and lovely views over the countryside to the south. Both cottages, each of which has its own garden furniture, have access to nearly an acre of garden.

In the village itself is the Ringstead Gallery (see next entry) and, close by, the Gin Trap Inn providing real ale, good food and a large garden. Just up the road the Post Office Stores has an interesting antiques and crafts section, and the village also boasts an excellent Nursery. A whole host of other visitor attractions are just a short drive away: great expanses of sandy beaches skirting the coast all the way from the Nature Reserve at Snettisham Scalp to Holkham Bay; grand historic houses; sleepy villages that seem suspended in the 1950s rather than the 1990s; and a delightful gentle countryside criss-crossed by a cat's-cradle of waymarked paths. *Sedgeford Road Farm Holiday Cottages, Ringstead, Hunstanton, PE36 5JZ. Tel: 01485 525530*

Margaret and her husband Donald are also partners in the **Ringstead Gallery** which attracts discerning art lovers from across the country to this small village. The gallery stands in the centre of Ringstead, next door to the Gin Trap Inn and with the old village water pump a few yards from the front door. Donald and Margaret opened the gallery some 20 years ago in a lovely old traditional building with whitewashed stone walls, an upper level gallery and two display areas on the ground floor. Here you'll find an excellent choice of fine paintings by such artists as Laurie Williamson, Philip

Ringstead Gallery

Gardner, Peter Barker, Neil Cox and many more. Their paintings capture the essence of the beguiling Norfolk landscape of sea, marshes and gently rolling countryside. The Ringstead Gallery also displays an exciting range of striking bronzes, items of turned wood and a good selection of limited editions. If you are looking for an original creation to give a distinctive touch to your decor, or an imaginative gift, there's every chance that you will find it here. *The Ringstead Gallery, Ringstead, Hunstanton, PE36 5JZ. Tel: 01485 525316*

Holme next the Sea
Map 2 ref D1

3 miles NE of Hunstanton, off the A149

This otherwise unremarkable village is notable as the northern end of the **Peddar's Way**, the 50-mile pedestrian trail that starts at the Suffolk border near Thetford and, almost arrow-straight for much of its length, slices across northwest Norfolk to Holme with only an occasional deviation to negotiate a necessary ford or bridge. This determinedly straight route was already long-trodden for centuries before the Romans arrived, but they incorporated long stretches of it into their own network of roads. It was from the Latin word "pedester", pedestrian, that the route takes its name. With few gradients of any consequence to negotiate, the Peddar's Way is ideal for the casual walker.

At Holme, the Peddar's Way meets with the **Norfolk Coast Path**, a much more recent creation. Starting at Hunstanton, it closely follows the coastline for more than 40 miles before ending at Cromer.

Docking

Map 2 ref D2

9 miles SE of Hunstanton, on the B1454 & B1153

One of the larger inland villages, Docking was at one time called Dry Docking because, perched on a hilltop 300ft above sea level, it had no water supply of its own. The nearest permanent stream was at Fring, almost 3 miles away, so in 1760 the villagers began boring for a well. They had to dig some 230ft down before they finally struck water which was then sold at a farthing (0.6p) per bucket. A pump was installed in 1928 but a mains supply didn't reach Docking until the 1930s.

On the edge of the village is ***The Pilgrim's Reach Restaurant***, certainly worth a pilgrimage for its alluring food, fine wines, attentive service and relaxing atmosphere. It's owned and run by James Lee and Sally Mash, two young and enthusiastic hosts who in a very short time have made The Pilgrim's Reach a "must-visit" restaurant for anyone in the area. Although widely-travelled, James is locally born and bred and delighted that he is now running a suc-

The Pilgrim's Reach Restaurant

cessful business in "his own backyard". The restaurant is housed in a traditional Norfolk building of stone, chalk and flint, parts of which are believed to date back to the 1500s. The interior is decorated with some fascinating local memorabilia: old hand tools, eel picks, the tools of the shepherd's trade, old implements used by marshmen and thatchers, all relating to a bygone Norfolk when life was lived at a gentler pace. A collection of old photographs of wherries and punts on the Norfolk Broads, and sailing vessels and lifeboats on the Norfolk coast enhance the strong "local flavour". Flavours of a different kind are evoked by the quite outstanding menu in which fish dishes have pride of place, - grilled Lowestoft cod fillet with pesto, pinenuts and prawns, for example, or escalopes of local Grey Mullet topped with pan-fried citrus prawns and cockles. If mussels are on the menu, only a couple of hours may have elapsed between them being harvested and their being served. If your preference is for meat, poultry or vegetarian dishes, you'll also find a good selection to choose from. The Bar Snacks menu shows the same inventiveness and concern with top-quality ingredients, meticulously prepared, and a great deal of expert knowledge has shaped the wine list, with wines supplied by Adnams, consistent winners of the National Wine Merchants of the Year Award. Should you find yourself anywhere near the Pilgrim's Reach, this is definitely a Hidden Place you should seek out. *The Pilgrim's Reach Restaurant, High Street, Docking, PE31 8NH. Tel: 01485 518383*

Standing in the heart of the village, ***Bakers Cottage*** is an appealing old house with primrose-painted walls and tubs of flowers flanking the doorway. As you might guess from the name, this was once the village bakery and its history stretches back to the 1600s. It is now a delightful guest house where Barbara Krauss and her friend Holly (an 8-year-old Labrador) give visitors a warm welcome. The cottage has been very sensitively refurbished, with the old

Bakers Cottage

beamed ceilings retained and with three wood-burning stoves creating a very cosy atmosphere. Lots of paintings, prints and curios
add to the inviting ambience, and the 3 twin bedrooms are furnished
and decorated with great taste. There's also a visitors' TV lounge
with a pleasant view across the garden.

Barbara is a talented craftswoman, making an attractive range
of cushions, lavender teddies, Peg Dolls, and dog and cat doorstops.
You'll find them on sale nearby at "Collectables" which is run by
Barbara's daughter and stocks a huge range of fascinating bygones.
There's anything from old paintings, prints and photographs to
kitchenware and linens; from vintage advertising artefacts to books
and magazines; from pine and oak county furniture to ephemera
and curios. A wonderful place to browse. *Bakers Cottage, Station
Road, Docking, King's Lynn, PE31 8LR. Tel: 01485 518710*

A couple of miles south of Docking stands the 5-storied **Great
Bircham Windmill**, one of the few in Norfolk to have found a hill
to perch on, and it's still working. If you arrive on a day when there's
a stiff breeze blowing, the windmill's great arms will be groaning
around; on calm days, content yourself with tea and home-made
cakes in the tea room, and take home some bread baked at the Mill's
own bakery.

Titchwell   Map 2 ref D1
7 miles E of Hunstanton, on the A149
Perhaps in keeping with the village's name, the **Church of St Mary**
at Titchwell is quite tiny, and very pretty indeed. Its circular, probably Norman, tower is topped by a little "whisker" of a spire, and
inside is some fine late 19th century glass. Just to the west of the
village is a path leading to **Titchwell Marsh**, a nationally important RSPB reserve comprising some 420 acres of shingle beach, reed
beds, freshwater and salt-marsh. These different habitats encour-
age a wide variety of birds to visit the area throughout the year, and
many of them breed on or around the reserve. Brent geese, ringed
plovers, marsh harriers, terns, waders and shore larks may all be
seen, and two of the three hides available are accessible to wheel-
chairs.

Brancaster Staithe   Map 2 ref E1
9 miles NE of Hunstanton, on the A149
In Roman times a castle was built near Brancaster to try and control the Iceni, Boadicea's turbulent tribe. Nothing of it remains,
although a Romano-British cemetery was discovered nearby in 1960.

In the 18th century, this delightful village was a port of some standing, hence the "Staithe", or quay, in its name. The waterborne traffic in the harbour is now almost exclusively pleasure craft, although whelks are still dredged from the sea bed, 15 miles out, and mussels are farmed in the harbour itself.

From the harbour, a short boat trip will take you to Scolt Head Island (National Trust), a 3½ mile sand and shingle bar separated from the mainland by a narrow tidal creek. It was originally much smaller but throughout the centuries deposits of silt and sand have steadily increased its size, and continue to do so. Scolt Head is home to England's largest colony of Sandwich terns who flock here to breed during May, June and July. A Nature Trail leads past the ternery, (closed during the breeding season), and on to a fascinating area where a rich variety of plantlife and wildlife abounds. During the summer, the sea asters, sea lavender and sea pinks put on a colourful display, attracting many different types of moths and butterflies.

The north Norfolk coast is famed for the abundance and variety of the birds to be seen there, and *The Jolly Sailors* at Brancaster Staithe is equally renowned amongst twitchers for the quality of its food, its warm, cosy atmosphere, and its services to bird-watchers. The inn is owned by Linda Murray, - young, enthusiastic and a pas-

The Jolly Sailors

sionate twitcher herself. A large blackboard outside lists current sightings: a siskin at Holme Observatory, a laughing gull at Titchwell, a grasshopper warbler at Barrow Common, perhaps. It's not only birds which are taken seriously here: the food served in the two restaurants (one is non-smoking) is also very customer-friendly.

The Jolly Sailors is open every day, all day from 8.00am, serving all day breakfasts (with porridge, and/or smoked kippers, if you wish), snacks, sandwiches and traditional home made meals until late in the evening. Fish, of course, is a speciality of the house with the day's fresh catch listed on the blackboard. And if you are planning a long day in the hides, The Jolly Sailors can also supply you with a packed lunch.

Children have their own menu (which includes Fish Whales) and a play area in the large garden. Not only are children welcome, so too, Linda says, are dogs and muddy boots! This informal atmosphere, along with the good range of real ales and an excellent selection of wines, all contribute to the popularity of this exceptionally appealing hostelry. Also not to be forgotten is the inn's great value-for-money Sunday roast served with Yorkshire Pudding and all the trimmings, (booking recommended). One more thing: if you are planning to stay in the area, The Jolly Sailors can also arrange accommodation. Just about the only thing they can't arrange, it seems, is to ensure you finally get to see that one elusive bird you want to tick off your list. *The Jolly Sailors, Main Road, Brancaster Staithe, PE31 8BJ. Tel: 01485 210314*

Burnham Market
Map 2 ref E1

9 miles E of Hunstanton, on the B1155

There are seven Burnhams in all, strung along the valley of the little River Burn. Burnham Market is the largest of them, its past importance reflected in the wealth of Georgian buildings surrounding the green, and the two churches that lie at each end of its broad main street, just 600 yards apart. In the opinion of many, Burnham Market has the best collection of small Georgian houses in Norfolk and it's a delight to wander through the yards and alleys that link the town's three east-west streets.

Lying so close to the coast, it's appropriate that Burnham Market should be able to boast one of the best sea food restaurants in the country, *Fishes*. This superb eating place specialises in fresh local sea food, including shellfish, shrimps from the Wash, lobster (when available), and fish landed on the beach at nearby Holkham Bay. Starters include crab soup, smoked fish pâté, and Brancaster oysters, as well as interesting non-fish choices such as goat cheese with asparagus vinaigrette. The enticing main dishes range from salmon fishcakes with crab sauce to a Crustacean Plate of lobster, crab, prawns, shrimps and crevettes, but you could also have home-baked ham with shrimp and parsley sauce. There's a separate menu for desserts (which include some delicious home-made puddings),

The Fishes' Restaurant

and smaller portions are available for children. The impressive 6-page wine list embraces selections from both Europe and the New World. In the 25 years that proprietor Gillian Cape has run Fishes she has maintained an enviable reputation for fine food, excellent service and outstanding value for money. Her restaurant, with its Victorian-style large-windowed double frontage, has a charming atmosphere, with comfortable cane furniture, attractive prints and paintings on the walls, and a fascinating collection of books. If you are a keen rambler, you will find that Gillian is a kindred spirit. An inveterate, experienced and indefatigable walker, Gillian has participated in the Mount Everest Base Trek and also travelled on foot through such exotic locations as Laos and Vietnam. Following the Norfolk Coastal Footpath, which passes nearby, must seem rather unadventurous in comparison but, as anyone who has walked even part of its 40-mile length will confirm, the footpath is by far the best way of getting to know this beguiling part of the county. *Fishes, Market Place, Burnham Market, North Norfolk, PE31 8HE. Tel: 01328 738588*

Burnham Thorpe   *Map 2 ref E2*
11 miles E of Hunstanton, on minor road off the B1355
From the tower of All Saints' Church, the White Ensign flaps in the breeze; the only pub in the village is the *Lord Nelson*; and the shop next door to it is called the Trafalgar Stores. No prizes for deducing that Burnham Thorpe was the birthplace of Horatio Nelson. His father, the Revd Edmund Nelson was the Rector here for 46 years and Horatio was the sixth of his eleven children.

Parsonage House, where he was born seven weeks premature in 1758, was demolished during his lifetime but the pub, (one of more than 200 hostelries across the country bearing the hero's name), has become a kind of shrine to Nelson's memory, its walls covered with portraits, battle scenes and other marine paintings.

There's more Nelson memorabilia in the church, amongst them a crucifix and lectern made with wood from *HMS Victory*; a great chest from the pulpit used by his father; and two flags from *HMS Nelson*. Every year on Trafalgar Day, October 21st, members of the Nelson Society gather at this riverside church for a service in commemoration of the man who had specified in his will that he wanted to be buried in its country graveyard, "unless the King decrees otherwise". George III did indeed decree otherwise and the great hero was interred in St Paul's Cathedral.

A little over a mile to the south of Burnham Thorpe stand the picturesque ruins of Creake Abbey (English Heritage, free), an Augustinian monastery founded in 1206. The Abbey's working life came to an abrupt end in 1504 when, within a single week, every one of the monks died of the plague.

Holkham
Map 2 ref F1

16 miles E of Hunstanton, on the A149

If the concept of the Grand Tour ever needed any justification, **Holkham Hall** amply provides it. For six years, from 1712 to 1718, young Thomas Coke (pronounced Cook) travelled extensively in Italy, France and Germany, studying and absorbing at first hand the glories of European civilisation. And, wherever possible, buying them. When he returned to England, Coke realised that his family's modest Elizabethan manor could not possibly house the collection of treasures he had amassed. The manor would have to be demolished and a more worthy building erected in its place.

During his travels in Italy, Coke had been deeply impressed by the cool, classical lines favoured by the Renaissance architect, Andrea Palladio. Working with his friend Lord Burlington, - another fervent admirer of Palladio, and the architect William Kent, Coke's monumental project slowly took shape. Building began in 1734 but was not completed until 1762, three years after Coke's death.

The completed building, its classical balance and restraint emphasised by the pale honey local brick used throughout, has been described as *"the ultimate achievement of the English Palladian movement"*. As you step into the stunning entrance hall, the tone is set for the rest of the house. Modelled on a Roman Temple of Jus-

Holkham Hall

tice, the lofty coved ceiling is supported by 18 huge fluted columns of pink Derbyshire alabaster transported to nearby Wells by river and sea.

Historically, the most important room at Holkham is the Statue Gallery which contains one of the finest collections of classical sculpture still in private ownership. In this sparsely furnished room there is nothing to distract one's attention from the sublime statuary that has survived for millennia, amongst them a bust of Thucydides, (one of the earliest portrayals of man), and a statue of Diana, both of which have been dated to 4 BC.

Each room reveals new treasures: Rubens and Van Dyck in the Saloon (the principal reception room); the Landscape Room with its incomparable collection of paintings by Lorrain, Poussin and other masters; the Brussels tapestries in the State Sitting Room; and, on a more domestic note, the vast, high-ceilinged Kitchen which remained in use until 1939 and still displays the original pots and pans.

Astonishingly, the interior of the house remains almost exactly as Thomas Coke planned it, his descendants having respected the integrity of his vision. They concentrated their reforming zeal on improving the enormous estate and it was Coke's great-nephew, Thomas William Coke (1754-1842), in particular who was responsible for the elegant layout of the 3000 acre park we see today. Universally known as "Coke of Norfolk", Thomas was a pioneer of the Agricultural Revolution, best known for introducing the idea of a four-crop rotation. He was also a generous patron of agricultural innovations and the "Sheep Shearings" he inaugurated, - gatherings to which several hundred people came to exchange ideas on all aspects of agriculture, were the direct forerunners of the modern agricultural show.

The Thomas Coke who built the house had been created Earl of Leicester in 1744, but as his only son died before him, the title lapsed. However, when his grand-nephew, "Coke of Norfolk", was elevated to the peerage by Queen Victoria in 1837 he adopted the same title. The present Earl, the 7th of the second creation, lives at Holkham in the private apartments known as the Family Wing but still uses the State Rooms when entertaining guests. The Earl continues in the tradition of "Coke of Norfolk" by overseeing the vast estate with its 30 tenant farmers and more than 300 houses: the Countess has established a new tradition by setting up the Holkham Pottery in the former brickworks.

As well as the Pottery and its associated shop, Holkham's other attractions include an 18th century Walled Garden, a fascinating Bygones Museum, a Garden Centre, Gift Shop and Tea Room. Tel: 01328 710227

Wells-next-the-Sea
Map 2 ref F1
17 miles E of Hunstanton, on the A149

It's difficult to decide whether Wells is a small town or a large village, but there's no doubt about the appeal of its picturesque quayside, narrow streets and ancient houses. Wells has been a working port since at least the 13th century but over the years the town's full name of Wells-next-the-Sea has become increasingly inapt, - its harbour now stands more than a mile from the sea. In 1859, to prevent the harbour silting up altogether, Lord Leicester of Holkham Hall built an Embankment cutting off some 600 acres of marshland. This now provides a pleasant walk down to the sea.

The Embankment gave no protection however against the great floods of 1953 and 1978. On the 11th January, 1978, the sea rose 16ft 1in above high tide, a few inches less than the 16ft 10in recorded on the 31st January, 1953 when the flood-waters lifted a ship on to the quay. A silo on the harbour is marked with these abnormal levels.

Running alongside the Embankment is the **Harbour Railway**, which trundles from the small Museum on the quay to the lifeboat station by the beach. This narrow-gauge railway is operated by the same company as the **Wells & Walsingham Light Railway** which carries passengers on a particularly lovely ride along the route of the former Great Eastern Railway to Little Walsingham. The 4-mile journey takes about 25 minutes with stops at Warham St Mary and

Wighton. (For timetable details, call 01328 856506). Both the WWLR and the Harbour Railway services are seasonal. In a curious change of function, the former GER station at Wells is now home to the well-known Burnham Pottery, the former signal box is now the station, while the old station at Walsingham is now a church!

In addition to being the largest of North Norfolk's ports, Wells is also a popular resort with one of the best beaches in England bordered by the curiously named ***Holkham Meals***, a plantation of pines established here in the 1860s to stabilise the dunes.

On the outskirts of the town, ***The Old Rectory*** offers visitors an interesting variety of holiday accommodation. The handsome 200-year-old building is set in secluded grounds of approximately 3 acres, a formerly wooded area which has been replanted with areas of grass, orchard and paddocks. In the house itself, the former servants' quarters have been converted into an attractive, fully equipped two-storey apartment with two bedrooms, sleeping 4/5 people. Adjacent to the house, the first floor area above the former coach house and tack room has been recently converted into a Studio Flat. Newly equipped, the flat has many charming features, - exposed low beams and ceilings, and dormer windows facing east overlooking the Old Rectory grounds. There's a twin bedroom and a modern double sofa bed in the open plan living room. Guests have the use of a modern outdoor heated swimming pool during the season by arrangement.

Sheila Griffiths-Jones can also offer visitors alternative accommodation about 150 yards away, at Cadamy's Yard. The yard takes its name from the Cadamy family who moved to Wells in 1879 and set up a blacksmith's shop here. Since then the yard has seen many businesses come and go and has now been developed for residential

The Old Rectory

use, with three newly built cottages and two flats on the site. Numbers 1 to 3 are small flint and brick-faced cottages built in the traditional style of older properties found around the town. Each cottage sleeps 5 people. Numbers 4 and 5 are first floor flats which are timber boarded above brickwork to garages beneath and the effect is of a fisherman's loft, reflecting part of the history of the town of Wells. All properties are newly constructed, attractively furnished, and equipped to a very high standard. (Please note that pets are not allowed in any of The Old Rectory properties). *The Old Rectory, Church Street, Wells-next-the-Sea, NR23 1JB. Tel: 01328 710858*

CHAPTER SIX
In and Around Fakenham

'The Clink' at Little Walsingham

Chapter 6 - Area Covered

For precise location of places please refer to the colour maps found at the rear of the book.

6
In & Around Fakenham

Introduction

Within a radius of a few miles from the small town of Fakenham can be found a remarkable variety of places of interest. To the north, in the valley of the River Stiffkey, the Shrine of Our Lady of Walsingham was in medieval times second only to that of Thomas à Becket at Canterbury as a pilgrim destination. To the northeast, the Thursford Collection is home to an astonishing gathering of steam-powered engines of every description, including a monumental Wurlitzer organ. On the eastern outskirts of the town, you can visit the premier collection of endangered and exotic waterbirds to be found in Europe, and over to the west stands the Marquess of Cholmondely's majestic home, Houghton Hall. More than enough to keep you occupied for a few days!

Fakenham   *Map 2 ref F3*
25 miles NW of Norwich, on the A1067/A148
Fakenham is a busy and prosperous-looking market town, famous for its National Hunt Racecourse, antique & bric-a-brac markets and auctions, and as a major agricultural centre for the region. Straddling the River Wensum, this attractive country town has a number of fine late-18th and early-19th century brick buildings in and around the Market Place. And it must surely be one of the few towns in England whose the former gasworks (still intact) has been turned into a ***Museum of Gas & Local History***, housing an impressive historical display of domestic gas appliances of every kind. Fakenham Church also has an unusual feature, a powder room, - although the

room over the large porch, built in 1497, was used for storing gunpowder rather than cosmetics. Even older than the church is the 700 year-old hunting lodge, built for the Duchy of Lancaster, which is now part of the Crown Hotel.

As an antidote to the idea that Norfolk is unremittingly flat, take the B1105 north out of Fakenham and after about half a mile take the first minor road to the left. This quiet road loops over and around the rolling hills, a ten-mile drive of wonderfully soothing countryside that only ends at Wells-next-the-Sea.

Southeast of Fakenham, off the A1067, **Pensthorpe Waterfowl Park** is home to Europe's best collection of endangered and exotic waterbirds. Over 120 species of waterfowl can be seen

Fakenham Market Place

here in their natural surroundings, a wonderful avian refuge where you may come across anything from a scarlet ibis to the more familiar oystercatcher, along with avocets and ruff. The spacious walk-through enclosures offer close contact with shy wading birds, and in the Dulverton Aviary elegant spoonbills and bearded tits vie for your attention. There are good facilities for the disabled and children, a Wildlife Brass Rubbing Centre, nature trails through 200 acres of the Wensum Valley countryside, a restaurant, and shop. Tel: 01328 851465.

Great Snoring
Map 2 ref G3
5 miles NE of Fakenham, on minor road off the A148
The names of the twin villages, Great and Little Snoring, are such a perennial source of amusement to visitors it seems almost churlish

to explain that they are derived from a Saxon family called Snear. At Great Snoring, the main street rises from a bridge over the River Stiffkey and climbs up to St Mary's Church. Just across from the church, is **The Old Rectory**, an exceptionally handsome Tudor manor house, a beguiling medley of gables, panelled turrets, grouped columns of chimneys, and mellow decorated brickwork. The house was built in the reign of Henry VIII by Sir Ralph Shelton, and on the south-east façade the stone mullioned windows are bordered with frieze designs in terracotta tiles which include alternate male and female heads, believed to represent members of the Shelton family. Others show the Shelton rebus and heraldic shield which is also carved on the oak front door.

The Old Rectory

The original building was in the unusual shape of a hexagon, but during restoration and development in the Victorian period the house was extended and assumed its present form. Today, this lovely old house, which stands in one and a half acres of walled garden, offers an excellent standard of accommodation with comfortable, well-equipped bedrooms, all en suite. The tariff includes early morning tea served in your room, and an excellent breakfast. Mid-morning coffee, luncheon hampers, afternoon tea, and dinner are also available. Recommended by a whole shelf-full of guide books, amongst them Egon Ronay, Michelin, The Good Hotel Guide, and Best Loved Hotels of the World, the Old Rectory conjures up "a pastoral idyll, a retreat from the cares of the world". Its location provides easy access to Norwich and King's Lynn with their historical, cultural and commercial interest, and to the heritage coast for fresh air, freedom and wide open spaces. The county's historic houses, busy little market towns and picturesque villages are all within easy reach, making this peaceful haven a delightful base for your exploration of Norfolk's Hidden Places. *The Old Rectory, Great Snoring, Fakenham, NR21 0HP. Tel: 01328 820597/Fax: 820048*

About 3 miles northeast of Great Snoring stands what is perhaps the most unusual museum in Norfolk, **The Thursford Collection**. George Cushing began this extraordinary collection of steam-powered traction engines, fairground organs and carousels back in 1946 when "one ton of tractor cost £1". Perhaps the most astonishing exhibit is a 1931 Wurlitzer organ whose 1,339 pipes can produce an amazing repertoire of sounds, - horses' hooves, fire engine sirens, claps of thunder, waves crashing on sand, and the toot-toot of an old railway engine are just some of the Wurlitzer's marvellous effects. There are regular live music shows when the Wurlitzer displays its virtuosity and other attractions include a steam-powered Venetian Gondola ride; shops selling a wide variety of goods, many of them locally made; and a tearoom. The museum is open daily from Easter to October, afternoons only: for more details, call 01328 878477.

A mile or so north of the Thursford museum, in the village of Hindringham, **Mill Farm Rare Breeds** is home to dozens of cattle, sheep, pigs, goats, ponies, poultry and waterfowl which were once commonplace but are now very rare. These intriguing creatures have some 30 acres of lovely countryside to roam around. Children are encouraged to feed the animals and there's also an Adventure Playground, crazy golf course, craft & gift shop, picnic area and tearoom. For further details, telephone 01328 878560.

Little Walsingham
Map 2 ref F2

5 miles N of Fakenham, on the B1105

Every year, some half a million pilgrims make their way to this little village of just over 500 souls to worship at the **Shrine of Our Lady of Walsingham**. In 1061 the Lady of the Manor of Walsingham, Lady Richeldis de Faverches, had a vision of the Holy Virgin in which she was instructed to build a replica of the Holy House in Nazareth, the house in which the Archangel Gabriel had told Mary that she would be the mother of Christ. Archaeologists have located the original house erected by Lady Richeldis. It was just 13ft by 23ft and made of wood, later to be enclosed in stone.

These were the years of the Crusades, and the **Holy House** at Walsingham soon became a major centre of pilgrimage, because it was regarded by the pious as an authentic piece of the Holy Land. Around 1153, an **Augustinian Priory** was established to protect the shrine, now encrusted with jewels, gold and silver, and to provide accommodation for the pilgrims. The Priory is in ruins now but the largest surviving part, a stately Gatehouse on the east side of the High Street is very impressive.

For almost 500 years, Walsingham prospered. Erasmus of Rotterdam visited in 1511 and was critical of the rampant commercialisation of the Shrine with its plethora of bogus relics and religious souvenirs for sale. He was shown a gigantic bone, "the finger-joint of St Peter" no less, and in return for a small piece of translation was presented with a highly aromatic fragment of wood, - a sliver of a bench on which the Virgin had once seated herself.

In the same year that Erasmus visited, Henry VIII also made the pilgrimage that all his royal predecessors since Richard I had undertaken. He stayed overnight at the enchanting early-Tudor mansion, **East Barsham Hall**, a glorious medley of mullioned windows, towers, turrets, and a group of 10 chimneys, each one individually carved with an amazing variety of styles. Since the King's visit, the Hall has had a succession of owners over the years, amongst them a Hapsburg Duke who entertained his neighbours in truly Imperial style before disappearing leaving behind some truly Imperial debts, and the pop group, the "Bee Gees". The Hall is today owned by a London businessman and not open to the public, but it stands for all to see as you enter the village.

After his overnight stay at East Barsham Hall, Henry VIII, like most other pilgrims, went first to the **Slipper Chapel**, a beautiful 14th century building about a mile away in Houghton St Giles. Here he removed his shoes and completed the last stretch on foot. Despite this show of piety, some 25 years later Henry had no hesitation in closing the Priory along with all the other monastic institutions in his realm, seizing its treasures and endowments, and having its image of the Virgin publicly burnt at Chelsea.

Little Walsingham itself is an exceptionally attractive village, set in the midst of parks and woodlands, and with fine medieval and Georgian houses lining its streets. Also of interest are the 16th century octagonal **Clink in Common Place**, used in medieval times as a lock-up for petty offenders; the scanty ruins of Walsingham's **Franciscan Friary** of 1347; and the former **Shire Hall** which is now a museum.

Clink in Common Place

Well-informed visitors to Little Walsingham will seek out Wendy and Titch Adams' splendid inn, the **Robin Hood**. They come not just for the good food and real ales at reasonable prices, but also to soak up the atmosphere created by the wonderful wall paintings depicting scenes from the life and times of the famous outlaw. Pictures, comic books and other Robin Hood memorabilia also celebrate the great legendary figure. Wendy and Titch both cook and their menu includes a tempting choice of fish, meat and vegetarian dishes. There's also a good selection of meat or fish salads, and if you are just looking for a snack, the fresh French flutes are ideal. They're baked on the premises daily and filled to your choice with meat, fish or cheeses. The curries, too, are highly recommended. Children are made welcome, and a selection of children's meals is always available.

The Robin Hood offers its guests a comprehensive wine list and for fairweather days, there's an attractive Beer Garden. Coffee, tea and snacks are served from 8 am, throughout the summer season, and at weekends the Adams lay on live music in the evenings. If you are planning to stay in the area, the Robin Hood has 4 attractive letting rooms, all recently refurbished. Two of them are en suite,

The Robin Hood Inn

the other two share a bathroom. The major attraction in the neigh-bourhood is, of course, the shrine which in medieval times was the second most important place of pilgrimage in England after Tho-mas à Becket's at Canterbury. But the village is also the southern terminus of the quaint miniature railway that runs up to the coast near Wells-next-the-Sea, and the great houses of Holkham Hall, Houghton Hall and Sandringham House are all within easy reach. *Robin Hood, Egmere Road, Little Walsingham, NR22 6BT. Tel: 01328 820252*

Great Walsingham
Map 2 ref G2

5 miles N of Fakenham, on the B1388

English place names observe a logic of their own, so Great Walsingham is of course smaller than Little Walsingham. The two villages are very different in atmosphere and appearance, Great Walsingham displaying the typical layout of a rural Norfolk settle-ment, with attractive cottages set around a green watered by the River Stiffkey, and dominated by a fine 14th century church, *St Peter's*, noted for its superb window tracery, wondrously carved Norman font, and perfectly preserved 15th century carved benches.

In a wonderfully peaceful location on the edge of the village, **Berry Hall** is the home of Joan Sheaf who welcomes visitors for bed and breakfast. The house is set in a lovely four-and-a-half acre garden. It was built for Thomas Berry in 1532 and its owners had close links with Matthew Parker, Archbishop of Canterbury in the reign of Elizabeth I. Much later, the family of Rupert Brooke, the World War I poet, lived here. There's also a tradition that George III had links with the family living here, but this has not yet been substantiated.

Today, Berry Hall is a warm, comfortable and much-loved family home, retaining many of its original features. There is a visitors' sitting room with a colour television and log fire in winter, a spacious dining room, and ample bathrooms and toilet facilities. The bedrooms are very comfortable, with duvets, electric blankets and early morning tea and coffee making facilities. Joan only has a few

Berry Hall

guests at a time in order to maintain the peaceful atmosphere of her home. Dinner is available and the food is plentiful and well-cooked, using fresh local produce. Please note that, owing to the great age of the house, smoking is not permitted.

Also available for self-catering holidays, is a charming single storey detached cottage situated at the entrance to Berry Hall. Attractively furnished, the cottage has two bedrooms, each with two single beds. Up to two well-behaved pets are welcome. Located just 4 miles from the beautiful North Norfolk coast, Berry Hall is also close to many places of interest. Little Walsingham, with its famous

Shrine and the remains of Walsingham Abbey, is close by, and such visitor attractions as Holkham Hall, Cley Mill, Langham Glass, and the market towns of Fakenham and Holt are all within easy reach. *Berry Hall, Great Walsingham, NR22 6DZ. Tel: 01328 820267*

Waterden   *Map 2 ref F2*
7 miles N of Fakenham, on minor road off the B1355

A farm, a tiny, towerless church, and **The Old Rectory**, - that's about all there is to this speck of a hamlet tucked away in the gentle Norfolk countryside. But if you are looking for a good place to stay for bed and breakfast hereabouts, The Old Rectory is well worth seeking out. Built in the 1840s, the spacious old house is surrounded by lovely gardens, both formal and natural, and the owner Rosemary Pile makes sure that guests are very well looked after. There's

The Old Rectory

a welcoming log fire in the guests' drawing-room and the three bedrooms, all twin or double, and all en suite, are attractively furnished and fully equipped. One of the bedrooms is on the ground floor, with French doors opening on to the garden, and is suitable for disabled visitors. The Old Rectory used to serve All Saints Church, a stone's throw away. This minuscule but appealing building is now in the care of English Heritage. *The Old Rectory, Waterden, Walsingham, NR22 6AT. Tel: 01328 823298*

Wighton   *Map 2 ref G2*
7 miles N of Fakenham, on the B1105

Wighton Post Office must be one of very few in the country where you can buy a postal order and a pint at the same time. This happy

The Carpenters Arms

state of affairs has come about because the post office desk is located in the bar of the village pub, ***The Carpenters Arms***. The desk is open two days a week and provides all the normal post office services apart from passports and Road Tax licences. This unusual arrangement, which has been featured on the TV programme, *Country File,* means that the Carpenters Arms is even more of a centre for village life than the traditional country pub. It's a free house, owned and run by a young and enthusiastic couple, Jason and Mandy Marsh.

When they took over, the pub was called The Sandpiper, but they have restored the name by which it has been known for most of its long history. Mandy looks after the kitchen and her menu offers an interesting and varied selection of home-cooked dishes, all prepared using the freshest of local produce. The frequently changing menu is complemented by an excellent choice of both regular and guest ales, alongside a wine list which is remarkable both for its variety and its outstanding value. There's a games room with pool and darts, and, outside, an attractive Beer Garden. *The Carpenters Arms, High Street, Wighton, Wells-next-the-Sea, NR23 1PF. Tel: 01328 820752*

Tatterford *Map 2 ref F3*

5 miles SW of Fakenham, on minor road off the A148 or A1065
This tiny village is well-known to botanists for ***Tatterford Common***, an unspoilt tract of rough heathland with tiny ponds, some

wild apple trees, and the River Tat running through it to join the River Wensum about a mile away.

On the outskirts of the village, ***Manor Farm Barn*** enjoys a wonderfully peaceful and relaxed setting for bed and breakfast or longer stays. The ingeniously converted barn, built of warm old brick, has hardwood floors and open rafters with a wealth of beams. The open plan design provides a very spacious living area and the two dual purpose bedrooms are absolutely huge. Each bedroom has a private bathroom and can be booked as either a family, double or single.

Manor Farm Barn

Manor Farm Barn is owned and run by Jane and Michael Davidson-Houghton who, in their four years here, have already attracted a loyal clientele, many of whom return again and again. Jane's background is in nursing, Michael's in the Royal Navy, and they both have a relaxed, unfussy style which makes for a restful and refreshing atmosphere. The tariff includes a hearty Norfolk breakfast and evening meals can be served by arrangement. Seafood, when available, is a popular item on the menu which generally favours traditional English cooking. Disabled guests can usually be accommodated, but a call is suggested to discuss any particular requirements. The old barn is surrounded by great vistas of open countryside with panoramic views extending for miles and miles, - a veritable little hamlet paradise! *Manor Farm Barn, Tatterford, nr Fakenham, NR21 7AZ. Tel: 01485 528393*

About 4 miles to the west of Tatterford stands ***Houghton Hall***, home of the Marquess of Cholmondely and one of Norfolk's most magnificent buildings. This glorious demi-palace was built in the Palladian style during the 1720s by Sir Robert Walpole, England's first Prime Minister. The Walpoles had been gentlemen of substance here since the 14th century. With his family revenues augmented by the considerable profits Sir Robert extracted from his political office, he was in a position to spend lavishly and ostentatiously on his new house. The first step was to completely destroy the village of Houghton, (it spoilt the view), and re-house the villagers a mile away at New Houghton.

Houghton Hall

Although Sir Robert deliberately cultivated the manner of a bluff, down-to-earth Norfolk squire, the personal decisions he made regarding the design and furnishings of the house reveal a man of deep culture and refined taste. It was he who insisted that the Hall could not be built in homely Norfolk brick, but in the whole of the county there is virtually no stone suitable for construction on this scale. The expensive decision was taken to use the exceptionally durable stone quarried at Aislaby in North Yorkshire, transporting it by sea from Whitby to King's Lynn. More than two and a half centuries later, the Aislaby stone is still flawless, the only sign of its age a slight weathering that has softened its colour to a creamy gold.

To decorate the interior and design the furniture, Sir Robert commissioned the versatile William Kent. Kent was at the peak of his powers, - just look at the decoration in the Stone Hall, the exquisite canopied bed in the Green Velvet Bedchamber, and the finely-carved woodwork throughout which made impressive use of the newly-discovered hardwood called mahogany. And then there were the paintings, an incomparable collection of Old Masters personally selected by Sir Robert. Sadly, many of them are now in the Hermitage Museum in St Petersburg, sold by his wastrel grandson to the Empress Catherine of Russia.

This grandson, George, 3rd Earl of Orford, succeeded to the title at the age of 21 and spent the next 40 years dissipating his enormous inheritance. When his uncle Horace, (the 4th Earl, but better known as Horace Walpole, novelist, MP, and inveterate gossip), succeeded to the title he found *"Houghton half a ruin...the two great staircases exposed to all weathers; every room in the wings rotting with wet; the park half-covered with nettles and weeds; mortgages swallowing the estate, and a debt of above £40,000".*

Houghton's decline was arrested when the Hall passed by marriage to the Marquess of Cholmondely, Lord Great Chamberlain, in 1797. But it wasn't until 1913, when George, later the 5th Marquess, moved into the house with his new wife, Sybil Sassoon, that Houghton was fully restored to its former state of grace. The depleted collection of paintings was augmented with fine works by Sir Joshua Reynolds and others from Cholmondely Castle in Cheshire, and the Marchioness introduced new collections of exquisite French furniture and porcelain.

One of the 6th Marquess' interests was military history, and in 1928 he began the astonishing Model Soldiers Collection now on display at Houghton. More than 20,000 perfectly preserved models are deployed in meticulous reconstructions of battles such as Culloden and Waterloo, and in one exhibit, recreating the Grand Review of the British Army in 1895, no fewer than 3,000 figures are on parade. For more details, telephone 01485 528569

East Raynham   *Map 2 ref F4*
3 miles SW of Fakenham, on the A1065

Little more than 6 miles from Houghton Hall, at East Raynham, is another superb Palladian mansion, ***Raynham Hall***, designed by Inigo Jones and with magnificent rooms created a century later by William Kent. The house is only open to the public by appointment since it is the private residence of the 7th Marquess of Townshend. It was his 18th century ancestor, the 2nd Viscount, (better known as "Turnip" Townshend), who revolutionised English agriculture by promoting the humble turnip as an effective means of reclaiming untended land, for feeding cattle in winter, and along with wheat, barley and clover, as part of the four year rotation of crops that provided a cycle of essential nutrients for the soil. The Townshend family have owned extensive estates in this area for centuries and in St Mary's Church there are some fine monuments to their ancestors, the oldest and most sumptuous of which commemorates Sir Roger who died in 1493.

Apple Blossom and Cherry Blossom are the two appealing names given to the holiday cottages which Susan Panter runs at *"Clebar"*. Each is set in about of an acre of landscaped gardens situated in a beautiful rural location offering a peaceful countryside holiday. Susan is a Yorkshire lass with a wonderful sense of humour and in the great traditions of Yorkshire hospitality makes sure that her visi-

"Clebar"

tors are as comfortable and well-looked after as it is possible to be. Apple Blossom cottage can sleep up to four people and a cot is available if required. Cherry Blossom sleeps just two in a double room: duvets and bed linen are provided. Both cottages have a lounge with colour TV, a fully equipped kitchen with fridge and microwave oven, and teatowels, dishcloths and table linen are provided. There's a shower room, where shower mats are provided though personal towels are required. The private patios overlooking the garden are fully equipped with garden furniture.

Susan also has a luxury mobile home to rent which can sleep up to four and is equipped to the same high standards as the two cottages. Accommodation is available all year round, usually on a weekly basis, but short breaks can also be arranged. In addition, the premises are licensed for 5 touring caravans and East Raynham's location in the heart of north Norfolk makes "Clebar" an ideal base for exploring this attractive part of the county. Sleepy villages, bustling market towns, historic houses and the magical north Norfolk coast are all within easy reach. *"Clebar", Colkirk Road, East Raynham, Fakenham, NR21 7EJ. Tel: 01328 855118*

CHAPTER SEVEN
Northeast Coast

Cley Mill

Chapter 7 - Area Covered

For precise location of places please refer to the colour maps found at the rear of the book.

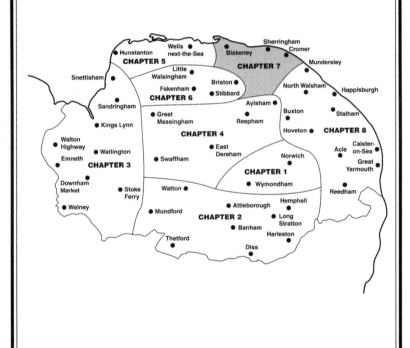

7
Northeast Coast

Introduction

As we travel eastwards from Wells, we are approaching the Highlands of Norfolk - the Cromer Ridge which attains the not very dizzying height of 330ft above sea level. The distance from Wells to Cromer is just over 20 miles but within that comparatively short length of coast, there's a dramatic change in its nature. If you stand on the low cliffs at Weybourne and look east, you are looking at a coastline that is constantly being eroded by the onslaught of tide and tempest. Look west and you will see a shoreline which, fed by the detritus of that erosion, is slowly pushing itself out into the sea. These marshy wetlands provide a perfect habitat for countless birds who in turn attract legions of twitchers armed, unlike their 19th century predecessors, with nothing more hostile than cameras and binoculars.

Substantial stretches of the coast between Wells and Sheringham are, happily, in the care of the National Trust, but anyone in search of a beach holiday will be much more interested in the coastline east of Sheringham. From this decorous resort, a broad strip of excellent sands runs almost uninterruptedly past Cromer and southwards to Great Yarmouth.

Wells-next-the-Sea has been described in an earlier chapter: we begin this one at the neighbouring village of Stiffkey.

Stiffkey   *Map 2 ref G1*
16 miles W of Cromer, on the A149
Regarded as one of the prettiest villages in the county, Stiffkey lies beside the little river of the same name. Pronounced "Stewkey", the

name means "island of tree stumps" and is most likely derived from the marshy river valley of reed beds and fallen trees which indeed gives the village the appearance of an island. At the east end of the village is the church of St John the Baptist and from the church-yard there are fine views of the river and of Stiffkey Hall to the south. All that now remains of this once-impressive building, built by the Bacon family in 1578, are the towers, one wing of the house, and the 17th century gatehouse. The stately ruins of the great hall have been transformed into a rose terrace and sunken garden and are open to the public.

The former Rectory is a grand Georgian building, famous as the residence of the Revd Harold Davidson, Rector of Stiffkey during the 1920s and 1930s. Rather like the central character in Michael Palin's film *The Missionary*, Harold launched a personal crusade to save the fallen women of London's West End, and caused much gossip and scandal by doing so. Despite the fact that his notoriety regularly filled the church to capacity, he constantly fell foul of the ecclesiastical authorities and eventually lost his living. There is a rather bizarre ending to his story. After handing over the keys of Stiffkey Rectory, Harold joined a travelling show and was later killed by a lion whose cage he was sharing.

To the north of the village are the **Stiffkey Salt Marshes**, a National Trust nature reserve which turns a delicate shade of purple in July when the sea lavender is in bloom. Here on the sandflats can be found the famous "Stewkey blues", - cockles which are highly regarded as a delicacy by connoisseurs of succulent bivalve molluscs.

A couple of miles south of Stiffkey stand the picturesque ruins of **Binham Priory** (English Heritage, free), its magnificent nave still serving as the parish church. This represents only about one-sixth of the original Priory, founded in 1091 by a nephew of William the Conqueror. The church is well worth a visit to see its unusually lofty interior with a Monk's Walk at roof level, its Seven Sacraments font, and noble west front.

Morston   Map 3 ref G1
13 miles W of Cromer, on the A149

Great stretches of salt marshes and mud flats lie between this pleas-ant village and the sea which is reached by way of a tidal creek that almost disappears at low tide. Morston is a particularly pleasing village with quiet lanes and clusters of cottages built from local cob-bles. If the church tower looks rather patched-up, that's because it was struck by lightning in 1743. It's said that local people took this as a sign that the Second Coming of Christ was imminent and that repairing their church was therefore pointless. It was many years before restoration work was finally undertaken, by which time the fabric of the tower had deteriorated even further.

A visit to **The Anchor pub** in Morston is an absolute must. This delightful old inn has been in the Temple family for more than a hundred years and although slightly updated in management, the bar rooms are relatively unchanged. Ann Temple was the original landlady and today you'll still find that most of the staff at The Anchor are Temples, or related! Jane and Jim Temple are the landlords, their daughter Louise is the chef and she produces a wonderful

The Anchor Pub

selection of home-made bar meals. The menu caters for all tastes, including vegetarians and children, and Louise has a very imaginative way with local fish and shellfish. People travel miles for her delicious mussels in garlic and white wine, and her crab dishes are just heavenly. There is always at least one real ale on offer, Wherry being the most popular. And, as Jim Temple points out, you are very likely to meet the locals while you are in The Anchor, so be prepared for the local dialect!

Jim is also a dedicated "boat man" and every day throughout the season his boats run from Morston Quay across Blakeney Harbour to see the colony of common and grey seals in their natural environment, basking on the sands around Blakeney Point. Whenever possible, visitors can also land on the Point, a National Trust Nature Reserve and the first to be established in Norfolk, back in 1912. You will see a wide variety of birds, there's a National Trust Information Centre to browse in, or you can simply enjoy drinks and snacks at the old lifeboat house. Combined with a visit to The Anchor, these seal trips, which last up to 2 hours, provide a splendid outing for adults and children alike. *The Anchor, The Street, Morston, nr Holt, NR25 7AA. Tel: 01263 740791*

The minor road leading south from Morston will bring you, after a mile or so, to **Langham Fine Norfolk Rural Crafts** where, in a wonderful collection of restored 18th century barn workshops, you watch a variety of craftspeople exercising their traditional skills. In addition to the now famous Langham Glass works where a master glass-maker will give a running commentary, there's a pyrographer, wood-turner, stained glass maker, and glass engraver. The Factory Gift Shop is well stocked with their creations, the Antiques & Collectables Shop offers a wide variety of items from Victorian china to Lalique, and there's also a Walled Garden, Adventure Playground and Restaurant. Tel: 01328 830511

Blakeney   *Map 3 ref H1*
14 miles W of Cromer, on the A149

One of the most enchanting of the North Norfolk coastal villages, Blakeney was a commercial port until the beginning of the 20th century when silting up of the estuary prevented all but pleasure craft from gaining access. The silting has left a fascinating landscape of serpentine creeks and channels twisting their way through

Seals at Blakeney Point

mud banks and sand hills. In a side street off the quay is the 14th century **Guildhall** (English Heritage; free), which was probably a private house and contains little of interest apart from the undercroft, or cellar, which is notable as an early example of a brick-built vaulted ceiling. The beautifully restored **Church of St Nicholas**, set on a hill overlooking village and marshland, offers much more to the visitor. The chancel, built in 1220, is lovely Early English work, and the magnificent west tower, 100ft high, is a landmark for miles around. In a small turret on the northeast corner of the chancel a light would once burn as a beacon to guide ships safely into Blakeney Harbour.

A short distance from the quay is **The Moorings Bistro and Tea Rooms**, owned and run by Ray Maddox. Manchester-born, Ray is a college trained chef with many years experience in London at the Cavendish Club and other venues where excellent cuisine is a matter of pride. He still visits London on a regular basis, picking up on the latest gastronomic trends. Ray came to Blakeney in 1995 and has transformed what was a simple tea room into a superb one and also introduced an evening bistro menu from Tuesday to Saturday.

The Moorings Bistro and Tea Rooms

The Tea Rooms are open every day serving light lunches, afternoon teas and Sunday lunch. There's a serene and friendly atmosphere in this charming old building with its flower-framed entrance, an ambiance enhanced on bistro evenings by an intriguing and lively menu complemented by an outstanding wine list. The adventurous menu changes every few weeks but, as an example, you might find Seared Yellow Fin Tuna with ratatouille, chilli and olive salsa amongst the starters, and a Roast Loin of Lamb with minted couscous listed in the main courses. A varied selection of desserts is displayed on the blackboard.

Each month, Ray arranges a variety of Gourmet Evenings when he undertakes some diverse and appealing themes. Past evenings have focussed on Thai, Italian, Mediterranean and Valentine themes. These gourmet evenings are understandably popular and it is strongly recommended that bookings are made as early as possible. *The Moorings Bistro & Tea Rooms, High Street, Blakeney, NR25 7NA. Tel: 01263 740054*

Cley-next-the-Sea   Map 3 ref H1
12 miles W of Cromer, on the A149

Like Wells-next-the-Sea, Cley's name is no longer appropriate. Cley-a-mile-away-from-the-Sea would be more truthful. But in early medieval times, Cley (pronounced Cly, and meaning clay) was a more important port than King's Lynn, with a busy trade exporting wool to the Netherlands. In return, Cley imported a predilection for houses with curved gables, Flemish bricks and pantiles. The windmill overlooking the harbour adds to the sense that a little piece of Holland has strayed across the North Sea. This is the famous *Cley Mill*, the subject of thousands of paintings. Built in 1713 and in use until 1921, the Mill is open to visitors during the season, (afternoons only), and also offers bed and breakfast.

The village's prosperity in the past is reflected in the enormous scale of its 14th/15th century parish church, *St Mary's*, whose south porch is particularly notable for its fine stonework and 16 armorial crests. The gorgeous fan-vaulted roof is decorated with bosses carved with angels, flowers, and a lively scene of an old woman throwing her distaff at a fox running away with her chickens.

From Cley, it's possible to walk along the shoreline to *Blakeney Point*, the most northerly extremity of East Anglia. This spit of land that stretches 3 miles out into the sea is a twitcher's paradise. Some 256 species of birds have been spotted here, and the variety of flora is scarcely less impressive: almost 200 flowering species have been recorded.

Cley Mill

About 2 miles south of Cley, near the delightful village of Glandford, the ***Natural Surroundings Wild Flower Centre*** is dedicated to gardening with a strong ecological emphasis. There are wild flower meadows and gardens, organic vegetable and herb gardens, nurseries, a nature trail alongside the unspoilt River Glaven, and the Centre also organises a wide range of events with a conservation theme. For more details, telephone 01263 711091. A short walk down the valley from the Centre is the ***Glandford Shell Museum***, a lovely Dutch-style building which houses the private collection of Sir Alfred Jodrell, a unique accumulation of sea shells gathered from beaches all around the world, together with a fascinating variety of artefacts made from them. The museum is open only during the summer months: for more details, telephone 01263 740081.

A couple of miles south of Glandford you'll find a building of 1802 which year after year has been awarded the title of *"Top Tourist Attraction in North Norfolk"*. ***Letheringsett Watermill*** stands on the site of an earlier mill recorded in the Doomsday Book and was rescued from near-dereliction in the 1980s. This fully functional, water-powered mill produces 100% wholewheat flour from locally grown wheat; there are regular demonstrations of the milling process, with a running commentary from the miller; and the end product can be purchased in the Gift Shop. For further information, phone 01263 713153.

Holt
Map 3 ref H2

10 miles SW of Cromer, on the A148

A perennial finalist in the Anglia in Bloom competition, Holt's town centre always looks a picture with hanging baskets and flowers everywhere. Back in 1892, a guide-book to the county described Holt as *"A clean and very prettily situated market town, being planted in a well undulating and very woody neighbourhood"*. More than a century later, one can't quarrel with that characterisation.

The worst day in the town's history was May 1st, 1708 when a raging fire consumed most of the town's ancient houses. The consequent rebuilding replaced them with some elegant Georgian houses, gracious buildings which played a large part in earning the town its designation as a Conservation Area.

The town's most famous building, **Gresham's School**, somehow escaped that disastrous conflagration of 1708. Founded in 1555 by Sir John Gresham, the school began as an altruistic educational establishment, its pupils accepted solely on the basis of their academic promise. Since then, the school has abandoned both its town centre location and its founder's commitment to educating, free, those bright children who could not otherwise afford it. Placing your child here, today, will drain more than £13,000 each year from your income. Solace yourself with the thought that amongst the school's many distinguished alumni are the dour creator of the BBC, Lord Reith, the poets W.H. Auden and Stephen Spender, and the composer Benjamin Britten.

Look out for one of Holt's most unusual buildings, **Home Place**. Designed and built in 1903-5 by E.S. Prior, an architect follower of the Arts & Crafts movement, the exterior of the house is completely covered with an ingeniously contrived cladding of local pebbles.

Enjoying a prime position on the High Street in Holt, **The King's Head** was named in honour of George III. The interior of this historic building has been recently refurbished by a conservationist designer, utilising period colours and features, and the overall effect is one of relaxation within the environment of a traditional hostelry. There are four eating areas: the lounge/restaurant; the

The King's Head

Maria Fitzherbert room (non-smoking); the Garden Room Restaurant; and the garden itself.

The pub's reputation for really excellent food is well-deserved, - the fare on offer providing a wonderful combination of the traditional, including vegetarian, and the unusual. The kitchen staff are delighted to prepare meals for any special dietary need and the wines are exceptionally good. Specially imported from wine-producing countries around the world, they represent remarkable value. If you prefer Real Ales, there are always 3 or 4 on tap, with at least one local brew. To complete the picture, there's a fine selection of keg and bottled beers to choose from.

The King's Head is a family pub, very "child-friendly" and with good access for the disabled. The easy, relaxed atmosphere is complemented by a willing and well-trained staff who appreciate old-fashioned values regarding service. Open all day, seven days a week, the King's Head is very popular with locals and tourists alike: - a wonderful place to have a morning coffee, lunch, or supper. Alternatively, just settle down with a fine pint, or glass of wine, and enjoy the good company and commodious surroundings.

Like the inn itself, many buildings in Holt date back to Georgian times, investing this small town with a gracious, almost stately, atmosphere. Crammed with antique and curiosity shops, Holt is also within easy reach of many of north Norfolk's most popular attractions, amongst them Holkham Hall, the Muckleburgh Collection of military memorabilia, the North Norfolk Railway and the Norfolk Shire Horse Centre. *King's Head, 19, High Street, Holt NR25 6BN Tel: 01263 712543*

About midway between Holt and Weybourne, in the grounds of the Kelling Park Hotel, is the **East Anglian Falconry Centre** which, in addition to having daily flying displays, is also the largest sanctuary in the country for injured owls and birds of prey. The centre keeps and cares for over 200 birds, amongst them kestrels and sparrowhawks, as well as a number of rarer birds such as goshawks, peregrine falcons, harriers and redtail hawks, eagle and snowy owls. The Centre is open daily all year, except Mondays during the winter months. Tel: 01263 712235.

Weybourne   *Map 3 ref I1*
9 miles W of Cromer, on the A149

Here, the shingle beach known as **Weybourne Hope** (or Hoop) slopes so steeply that an invading fleet could bring its ships right up to the shore. Which is exactly what the Danes did many times during the 9th and 10th centuries. A local adage states that *"He who would Old England win, Must at Weybourne Hoop begin"*, and over the centuries care has been taken to protect this stretch of the coast. A map dated 1st May 1588 clearly shows "Waborne Fort" and Holt's Parish Register for that year of the Armada notes that *"in this yeare was the town of Waborne fortified with a continuall garrison of men bothe of horse and foote with sconces (earthworks) ordinaunce and all manner of appoyntment to defend the Spannyards landing theare"*.

As it turned out, the Spannyards never got close, but during World Wars I and II the same concern was shown for defending this vulnerable beach. The garrison then became the Anti-Aircraft Permanent Range and Radar Training Wing, providing instruction for National Servicemen until the camp finally closed in 1959. It was reckoned that by then some 1,500,000 shells had been fired out to sea. The site has since been returned to agricultural use, but the original NAAFI building remains and now houses **The Muckleburgh Collection**, a fascinating museum of military vehicles, weapons, and equipment most of which has seen action in battlefields all over the world. All of the tanks, armoured cars, and amphibious vehicles on display can be inspected at close quarters, and there are regular tank demonstrations. (For details, call 01263 588210). Meals and snacks are available, - served in a NAAFI-style canteen.

Incidentally, despite Weybourne's exposed position, it has in fact only been attacked once, by the Luftwaffe on 11th July 1940. A stick of bombs landed in the main street and badly damaged two cottages.

About a mile from the village, *Weybourne Forest Lodges* occupy a particularly lovely and tranquil site. Lying within the North Norfolk Coast Area of Outstanding Natural Beauty, this small family-owned development is set in a peaceful glade within privately owned pine forest. The forest adjoins the National Trust-owned Sheringham Park and is perfect for walkers, bird watchers, nature lovers and horse riders - in fact, the Forest Lodge Riding School is actually on site and offers discounts to visitors staying at the lodges.

Weybourne Forest Lodges

The seven Scandinavian-style A-frame lodges are equipped to a very high standard, double-glazed and centrally heated, and each has its own large balcony. Another property, "Forest Villa", is a single storey holiday home with two double bedrooms. It has a ramp for wheelchair access but is not suitable for very handicapped people as there are no special facilities.

For a small charge, visitors to the lodges and "Forest Villa" can also enjoy unlimited use of the Pinewood Leisure Centre, a mile or so away, where the amenities include a 25-metre indoor heated swimming pool. Weybourne Forest Lodges are available to rent throughout the year, but please note that between May and the end of September bookings must be made through Hoseasons Holidays, (tel: 01502 500500).

The owners of Weybourne Forest Lodges, Chris and Joe Tansley, also have two other properties here for which bookings should be made directly with them. "Forest Chalet" is a cosy single storey pine chalet suitable for 2/4 people; "Chestnut Lodge" is a comfortable double-glazed Park Home sleeping 4/6 visitors. All the properties are spaced well apart and the 12-acre site provides a great play area for children, - and there's also a pets' corner. The North Norfolk railway runs through the fields below the forest to Weybourne Station and from there it's just one stop to Sheringham with its miles of superb beaches. *Weybourne Forest Lodges, Sandy Hill Lane, Weybourne, Holt, NR25 7HW. Tel: 01263 588440*

Surrounded by farm land, and with the sea as a soothing background, **Bolding Way Holiday Cottages** offers holiday-makers a choice of three outstandingly attractive self-catering properties. Located in a designated area of outstanding natural beauty, all three have been awarded the English Tourist Board's rating of 4 Keys Commended. Indeed, one of them, "The Cottage", which sleeps 8 + 2 + 2 cots, goes a step further with a 4 Keys *Highly* Commended accolade. This cottage dates back to 1604 and has been added to by each generation, giving this wonderful property a unique appearance. Until a few years ago, it was the home of the Harrison family who own these cottages and take a close personal interest in providing every possible help to ensure that visitors have a comfortable and relaxing holiday. "East Cottage" is another period property, dating from about 1880 when it was built as a nursery wing to The Cottage. Local people were particularly impressed by the fact that East Cottage included a bathroom, - only the second to be installed in the village. A charming building, constructed in traditional materials, East Cottage can sleep 6 plus 1 and cot. The third cottage, "The Coach House", is a former stable block, built in 1888 and converted in 1992 with some of its original features retained. An extension to the original building provides a spacious south-facing sitting-room, with wood panelled walls and a wood burner, overlooking its own enclosed sunny garden planted with fruit trees.

If you wish, an arrival pack of groceries can be arranged for you, but there's also a communal store, "Sagans", which, as well as pro-

Bolding Way Holiday Cottages

viding you with the wherewithal for an evening meal and break-fast, also has a video library, pay phone and much more. In addition, there are large communal gardens, shared by just the three cottages, and guests also have free membership of the Pinewood Park Leisure Club just three miles away. *Bolding Way Holiday Cottages, Bolding Way, Weybourne, nr Holt, NR25 7SW. Tel/Fax: 01263 588666*

Sheringham

Map 3 ref I1

5 miles W of Cromer, on the A149

Sheringham has made the transition from fishing village to popular seaside resort with grace and style. There are plenty of activities on offer but Sheringham has managed to avoid the brasher excesses of many English seaside towns. The beach here is among the cleanest in England and markedly different from the shingle beaches else-where on this part of the coast. Consisting mainly of gently sloping sand, it is excellent for bathing and the team of lifeguards makes it ideal for families with children. Rainfall at Sheringham is one of the lowest in the county and the bracing air has also recommended the town to sufferers from rheumatism and respiratory problems.

A small fleet of fishing boats still operates from here, mostly concentrating on crabs and lobsters, but also bringing in catches of cod, skate, plaice, mackerel and herring. Several original fishermens' cottages remain, some with lofts where the nets were mended. Sheringham has never had a harbour, so boats are launched from the shore where stacks of creels stand as they have for generations. A "golden lobster" in the town's coat of arms celebrates this traditional industry.

A mere three minutes walk from the sea, the town centre and the golf links, is the ***Southlands Hotel***, an impressive Edwardian building situated in quiet and pleasant surroundings. The hotel is under the personal supervision of its resident proprietors, Anthony and Estelle Preston, who provide elegant accommodation for their guests, with a delightful personal touch. They offer 17 comfortable bedrooms, all with bathrooms en suite and equipped with colour

The Southlands Hotel

television, tea and coffee-making facilities, hair dryers, and trouser presses. The dining rooms and bars offer an extensive choice in the best of English food, complemented with well-stocked bars. Although the Southlands Hotel is open to residents until the end of October, functions such as wedding receptions, conferences, and parties can be catered for throughout the year. *Southlands Hotel, South Street, Sheringham, NR26 8LL. Tel/Fax: 01263 822679*

Like so many other former fishing villages in England, Sheringham owes its transformation into a resort to the arrival of the railway. During the Edwardian peak years of rail travel, some 64 trains a day steamed into the station but the line became yet another victim of the Beeching closures of the 1960s. Devotees of

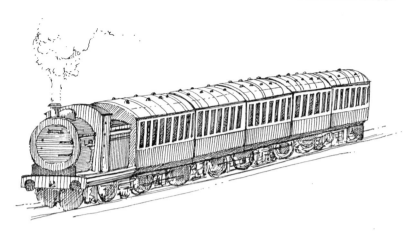

North Norfolk Railway

steam trains joined together and by dint of great effort and enthusiasm managed to re-open the line in 1975 as the **North Norfolk
Railway**, better known as **The Poppy Line**.

The name refers to Poppyland, a term given to the area by the
Victorian journalist Clement Scott who visited in pre-herbicide days
when the summer fields were ablaze with poppies. Although greatly
diminished in number, plenty of these brilliant flowers can still be
seen as you travel the scenic 5-mile journey from Sheringham to
Holt. The railway operates up to 8 trains daily in each direction
during the season, March to October, and there are special Saturday evening and Sunday lunchtime services when you can dine in
style in one of the Pullman coaches from the old "Brighton Belle".
For a talking timetable, call 01263 822045. *North Norfolk Railway,
The Station, Sheringham NR26 8RA Tel: 01263 822045*

On the outskirts of Sheringham is the **Pentland Lodge Guest
House** where a warm and friendly welcome awaits you, along with
wonderful food. The Lodge is just five minutes from the sea, ten
minutes from the town centre, and offers guests either full board or
just bed and breakfast. The five guest rooms here are much larger
than usual, the family rooms capable of accommodating two adults
and up to 3 or 4 children. The downstairs rooms are ideal for the
disabled and have their own ground floor toilet and shower. Pentland
Lodge is owned and run by Janet and John Nolson. John specialises
in the cooking, serving a good choice of beef, chicken, fish or vegetarian dishes. With advance notice, any special dietary
requirements can also be catered for. Janet, with many years craft

Pentland Lodge Guest House

and dressmaking experience, organises the popular Pentland Lodge Craft Holidays, with some courses held at weekends, others running from Monday to Friday. The choice of crafts is very wide and ranges from all forms of embroidery to parchment craft; from quilting and patchwork, and there are special Christmas Breaks where you can create your very own crackers, cards and Christmas decorations. *Pentland Lodge Guest House, 51, The Avenue, Sheringham, NR26 8DQ. Tel: 01263 823533*

Just to the west of the town, at Upper Sheringham, footpaths lead to the lovely grounds of **Sheringham Park** (National Trust). The Park was landscaped by Humphrey Repton who declared it to be his "favourite and darling child in Norfolk". There are grand views along the coast, dense growths of oak, beech and fir trees, and banks of rhododendrons which are at most dazzling in late May and June. Entrance is free for pedestrians, but if you want to drive, there's a pay car-park. There's yet more grand scenery at the aptly-named **Pretty Corner**, just to the east of the A1082 at its junction with the A148. This is a particularly beautiful area of woodland and also offers superb views over the surrounding countryside.

West Runton
Map 3 ref I1

3 miles W of Cromer, on the A149

The parish of West Runton can boast that within its boundaries lies the highest point in Norfolk, - **Beacon Hill**. This eminence is 330ft high so you won't be needing any oxygen equipment to reach the summit, but there are some excellent views and nearby is the Roman Camp (National Trust), a misleading name since there's no evidence that the Romans ever occupied this 70 acres of heathland. Excavations have shown, however, that in Saxon and medieval times this was an iron-working settlement.

Tucked away in the heart of the village, the ***Mirabelle Bistro and Restaurant*** offers visitors a mouth-watering menu of delicious dishes, many of them revealing an Austrian influence. Main courses such as Entrecôte Tyrolienne, Scampi or Chicken Viennoise, and Apple Strudel owe their continental flavour to owner/chef Manfred Holwogger who has been delighting customers here with his flair for cooking for more than 25 years. Amongst his other memorable specialities are melt-in-the-mouth Seafood Vol au Vents, pan fried salmon on a bed of Mediterranean char-grilled vegetables with a citrus sauce, and a lightly alcoholic Grand Marnier Soufflé. Manfred uses only the freshest and best ingredients available, - succulent meats, locally caught fish and seasonal vegetables and fruits. To complement the outstanding cuisine, the Mirabelle has a carefully chosen wine list featuring wines from almost every continent. Guests have the choice of eating either in the bistro, where the at-

Mirabelle Bistro and Restaurant

mosphere is less formal, or in the slightly formal restaurant where you can choose from the à la carte or restaurant menu. Whether you choose the bistro or the restaurant, you will find the food just as delicious in either. This exceptionally good eating place is open lunchtimes and evenings every day except Monday, and on Sunday evenings from November to May. *Mirabelle Bistro & Restaurant, Station Road, West Runton, Cromer, NR27 9QD. Tel: 01263 837396*

West Runton's major tourist attraction is undoubtedly the *Norfolk Shire Horse Centre* where twice a day, during the season, these noble beasts are harnessed up and give a half-hour demonstration of the important role they played in agricultural life right up until the 1930s. They are the largest (19 hands/6ft 4in high) and heaviest horses in the world, weighing more than a ton, and for generations were highly valued both as war-horses and draught animals. Several other heavy breeds, such as the Suffolk Punch, Clydesdale and Percheron, also have their home here, along with no fewer than 9 different breeds of pony. The Centre also has a video room showing a 30-minute film, a small animals' enclosure and an adventure playground for children, a cafe and gift shop. A horse-drawn cart will transport you around the village and at the West Runton Riding School (on site) you can hire riding horses by the hour. More details on 01263 837339.

If you enjoy food with a French flavour, then you should certainly seek out *The Pepperpot Restaurant* in a quiet little street called Water Lane. Antoine and Debbie Foucher have had over 15 years experience in England and France, working with the greatest chefs and in some of the finest establishments. From the outside, their white-painted restaurant with its window canopies, leaded glass windows and gabled entrance looks very inviting and the interior is no less attractive. There are, in fact, two restaurants here: the main restaurant seating 40, and the Garden Restaurant with covers for 25, with the same excellent food served in both.

Menus change daily to take advantage of the best fresh produce available, - especially the locally-caught fish. Amongst the starters you might find a Timbale of Wild Mushrooms, or Goat Cheese Provençale. The list of main courses always includes a vegetarian option along with outstanding dishes such as Pork Filet à la Normande and Breast of Chicken with Pink Berries. And for dessert, a difficult choice between Strawberry Charlotte, Chocolate & Orange Terrine or a selection of French and English cheeses served with biscuits and French bread. Everything on the menu, naturally, is home-made, and each meal is beautifully presented. West Runton

The Pepperpot Restaurant

is indeed lucky to have a restaurant offering such exquisite cuisine. *The Pepperpot Restaurant, Water Lane, West Runton, NR27 9QP. Tel: 01263 837578*

Aylmerton   *Map 3 ref I2*
3 miles SW of Cromer, on minor road off the A148

A couple of miles south of West Runton is one of Norfolk's grandest houses, *Felbrigg Hall* (National Trust). Thomas Windham began rebuilding the old manor house at Felbrigg in the 1620s, erecting in its place a grand Jacobean mansion with huge mullioned windows, pillared porch, and at roof-level a dedication in openwork stone: Gloria Deo in Excelsis, "Glory to God in the Highest". Later that century, Thomas' grandson William Windham I married a wealthy heiress and added the beautifully proportioned Carolean West Wing where visitors can see portraits of the happily married couple, painted by Sir Peter Lely. Their son, William Windham II, returning from his 4-year long Grand Tour, filled the house with treasures he had collected, - so many of them that he had to extend the Hall yet again. The Windham family's ownership of Felbrigg Hall came to a tragi-comic end in the 1860s when William Frederick Windham

Felbrigg Hall

inherited the estate. William was one of the great English eccentrics. He loved uniforms. Accoutred in the Felbrigg blue and red livery he would insist on serving at table; in guard's uniform he caused chaos on the local railway with his arbitrary whistle-blasts; dressed as a policeman, he sternly rounded up the ladies of easy virtue patrolling London's Haymarket. Inevitably, "Mad" Windham fell prey to a pretty fortune-hunter and Felbrigg was only saved from complete bankruptcy by his death at the age of 26.

The Hall was acquired by the National Trust in 1969, complete with its 18th century furnishings, collection of paintings by artists such as Kneller and van der Velde, and a wonderful Gothic library. There are extensive grounds which include a Walled Garden containing an elegant octagonal dove-house, an Orangery of 1707 sheltering an outstanding collection of camellias, many woodland and lakeside walks, a restaurant, tea room and shop. Tel: 01263 837444

Close to the southern boundary of Felbrigg Hall is **Felbrigg Lodge** which is designed to provide its guests with the highest possible standards of accommodation in North Norfolk, located in a setting which guarantees complete quiet and relaxation. Jill and Ian Gillam, who own and run this quite exceptional establishment, like to believe that Felbrigg Lodge offers a different concept of hospitality in an unbeatable rural setting, avoiding the impersonal and formal atmosphere of an hotel, and providing guests complete freedom to mix with others or to seek solitude as they choose.

Approached by a long private drive, the eight acres of grounds are wonderfully secluded and offer a true escape from the noise and bustle of modern day life. Here time has stood still, - nothing disturbs over 70 different species of birds and other wildlife amongst rolling lawns and specimen trees and shrubs. The rooms are sited around the grounds to take greatest advantage of the landscape and lovely views. All have been individually designed to the highest standards of decoration and appointment, and all have luxurious en suite bathrooms, colour television, and tea/coffee making facilities. Some have private terraces or gardens, and none of the rooms

Felbrigg Lodge

are close enough together to destroy the pervading sense of peace and tranquillity. Guests also have the use of a centrally placed and separate drawing room and dining room which they may use at any time, perhaps for a pre-dinner drink from the fully-stocked honesty bar. Other amenities include a full size billiard table, a heated indoor swimming pool (sometimes closed in winter), and a small well-equipped gym. For those who are more energetic, miles of traffic-free walking is possible through either the country lanes or the magnificent adjoining parkland of the Felbrigg Hall estate. *Felbrigg Lodge, Aylmerton, North Norfolk, NR11 8RA. Tel: 01263 837588*

Cromer

As you enter a seaside town, what more reassuring sight could there be than to see the pier still standing? ***Cromer Pier*** is the genuine article, complete with Lifeboat Station and the Pavilion Theatre which still stages traditional end-of-the-pier shows. The Pier's survival is all the more impressive since it was badly damaged in 1953 and 1989, and in 1993 sliced in two by a drilling rig which had broken adrift in a storm.

Cromer has been a significant resort since the late 1700s and in its early days even received an unsolicited testimonial from Jane Austen. In her novel "Emma" (1816) a character declares that "Perry was a week at Cromer once, and he holds it to be the best of all the sea-bathing places". A succession of celebrities, ranging from Lord Tennyson and Oscar Wilde to Winston Churchill and the German Kaiser, all came to see for themselves.

The inviting sandy beach remains much as they saw it, (horse-drawn bathing machines aside), and so does the **Church of St Peter & St Paul**, which boasts the tallest tower in Norfolk, 160ft high. And then as now, Cromer Crabs were reckoned to be the most succulent in England. During the season, between April and September, crab-boats are launched from the shore (there's no harbour here), sail out to the crab banks about 3 miles offshore, and there the two-man teams on each boat deal with some 200 pots.

The Lifeboat Museum, however, is a fairly recent addition. Housed in the former Lifeboat Station, it tells the dramatic story of the courageous men who manned the town's rescue service. Pre-eminent among them was Harry Blogg who was coxswain of the lifeboat for 37 years, from 1910 to 1947. During those years his boat, the *H F Bailey*, was called out 128 times and saved 518 lives. In 1991, the *H F Bailey* was purchased by Peter Cadbury of the chocolate manufacturing family and presented to the Museum as its prime exhibit.

Also well worth visiting is the **Cromer Museum**, housed in a row of restored fishermen's cottages near the church, where you can follow the story of Cromer from the days of the dinosaurs, some of whose bones were found nearby, up to the present, and access the computer for thousands of pictures and facts about this attractive town.

Occupying a prominent position on the seafront, the **Cliftonville Hotel** displays the stately Edwardian elegance so beloved by visitors to Cromer. But only a few years ago, in 1994, this grand old hotel was closed and boarded up. The Cliftonville was then purchased by Robert and Belinda Cammell who, together with Belinda's sister, Annette Grundy, refurbished the hotel to its former state of grace. The hotel's ground floor is dominated by a stunning staircase and classic stained glass, and upstairs, the 30 en suite bedrooms all enjoy excellent sea views. There's a choice of Family Suites, Executive Rooms, many pleasant single rooms, and a fabulous Honeymoon Suite with a king size brass bed, jacuzzi bath, and panoramic views.

The Cliftonville Hotel and Bolton's Bistro

The Cliftonville is a favourite venue for weddings, parties and dinners in either the sea-view Westcliff Dining Room, or in the Galleried Ballroom with its sprung dance floor, capable of accommodating up to 200 guests.

At the heart of the hotel is a dedication to quality food, with a focus on local seafood, so there are several eating areas to choose from. The Restaurant features a traditional table d'hôte menu, enhanced by a classic à la carte choice of dishes. In the Coffee Shop you'll find a full range of coffees and teas with La Patisserie offering pastries and cakes, freshly made sandwiches, hot baguettes and light meals. Especially popular is Bolton's Bistro, open every lunchtime from noon until 2.30 p.m. and every evening from 6 p.m. until 10 p.m. Fresh fish dishes, served with farm fresh vegetables, are a highlight of the menu with Cromer crabs and locally-caught lobsters always featured if they are available. Meat lovers and vegetarians are also well-catered for. Amongst other choices, there's always a Roast of the Day and vegetarian options include a Brie Cheese, Spinach & Tomato Bake. Whatever your preferences, you will find them completely fulfilled at this outstanding eating place. *Bolton's Bistro at the Cliftonville Hotel, Seafront, Cromer, NR27 9AS. Tel: 01263 512543*

Standing high on the cliffside, just 50 yards from the water's edge and overlooking the Pier, **The Dolphin Free House** is a substantial early Victorian building enjoying splendid views of the sea. Mick and Patricia Thomas have been here since 1991 and have a well-established reputation for the quality of their food, wines, and cask-conditioned ales and lagers. Their extensive menu includes a good selection of starters, salads, snacks, pasta and sandwiches or filled cobs. The main courses offer a choice of fish, vegetarian or meat dishes, and the desserts include old favourites like Spotted

The Dolphin Free House

Dick with creamy custard as well as some interestingly-named newer ones such as Chocka Rocka Cream Pie and Hankey Pankey Pie. The blackboard lists even more choices with a list of Daily Specials. Children are welcome at The Dolphin, or as Mick puts it, "Children with well-behaved parents" are! The menu includes a selection specially for them, there's a children's room next to the Sea View Restaurant, and baby changing facilities are also provided. On Sundays, in the non-smoking Restaurant, there's a Carvery with food served from noon until 9pm during July and August. (Throughout the rest of the year, the Carvery is open on Sundays only from noon until 2.30pm).

During the week, food is also available during July & August, from 12 noon until 9pm; in April, May, June & September it's served between 12 noon-2.30pm, and from 5.30pm -9.00 p.m. The Sea View Restaurant has become a popular venue for patrons of the Pier Show who come here to enjoy a pre-show meal. The Pier itself is a fine example of this attractive form of seaside architecture. It extends some 500ft into the sea, and is about 50 ft wide, with glass shelters providing protection from the wind for most of its length. Unlike many piers which are crowded with "amusements", Cromer's pier is a quiet, relaxing and refreshing place for a gentle walk, or perhaps a spot of fishing. *The Dolphin Free House, New Street, Cromer, NR27 9HP. Tel: 01263 512204/Fax: 515380*

Located in the centre of the town, ***Rumbletums Licensed Restaurant*** offers wholesome, varied food throughout the day and into the evening. Pam and Ted's family-friendly restaurant is open every day, all year round. They took over here and refurbished in 1996, Ted having been a decorator, Pam a supervisor in town planning, and immediately displayed a knack for running a successful restaurant where most of the fare is home made. A friendly staff maintains a high standard of service, and the prices reflect extremely good value for money. The *very* extensive menu offers a huge range of choices, from a simple, tasty sandwich, (Fresh Cromer Crab, for

Rumbletums Restaurant

example, when available), to hearty main courses such as hand made Steak, Mushroom and Guinness Pie, or a full, tender and juicy 8oz steak. There's an All Day Breakfast, fish and vegetarian options, a Cream Tea with home-made scone. Children have an unusually wide choice of meals, and desserts with gifts. The adult dessert menu is also wide-ranging with hot and cold choices, gateaux, and ice cream specialities such as Creme de Menthe Ice Cream Bombe.

Rumbletums is licensed to serve alcohol with main meals, with house wine, beers, spirits and connoisseur liqueur coffees all available to complement your food. Housed in a former shop with a traditional Victorian frontage, Rumbletums is accessible to the disabled, (although there is no disabled toilet). However, plans are under way and by the time you read this the new facilities may well be in place. With its convenient town centre location, Rumbletums is an ideal spot for refreshment, whether you are fresh from the beach, weary after some heavy shopping, or ready to relax and have a sociable evening meal. *Rumbletums Licensed Restaurant, 7, Hamilton Road, Cromer, NR27 9HL. Tel: 01263 514894*

CHAPTER EIGHT
Great Yarmouth and the Norfolk Broads

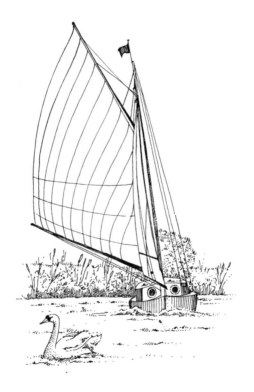

Museum of the Broads, Potter Heigham

Chapter 8 - Area Covered

For precise location of places please refer to the colour maps found at the rear of the book.

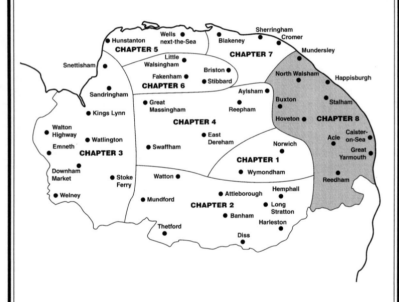

8
Great Yarmouth & the Norfolk Broads

Introduction

This chapter is devoted to a town which should be loved far more than it is, Great Yarmouth, and to a unique area of the country which is in serious danger of being loved to death, the Norfolk Broads. Too many people still regard Yarmouth as simply a brash, east coast clone of Blackpool, unaware of its long history as a major port, or of its many distinguished buildings. The town certainly has a dual-personality, and each of them has its own engaging and lively character.

To the north and west of Great Yarmouth lies the tourist honeypot of the Norfolk Broads. It's an area of outstanding natural beauty, but its beauty is desperately fragile. The constant wash from the wake of motor-boats has eroded the banks of its rivers and broad waters, clogging the shallow waterways with dislodged earth. The run-off from over-fertilized fields has fed a plague of algae which covers the waters and smothers to extinction the aquatic plants which were an important link in the food-chain supporting insects, fish and birds. Of the 46 bodies of water included in the Norfolk Broads, the Broads Authority declared in 1983 that only 4 were perfectly healthy, and a mere half a dozen others capable of supporting any plant life at all. The rest were biologically dead.

There is, however, an optimistic postscript to this dismal story. In 1988, the Norfolk Broads Authority was invested with the kind of powers enjoyed by National Parks to resist any further degradation of the area. The Authority's declared ambition is that by around the year 2050 they will have restored these lovely waterways to their erstwhile purity, an undertaking which it readily admits is "a marathon, not a sprint".

Great Yarmouth *Map 6 ref M6*

The topography of Great Yarmouth is rather curious. Back in Saxon times, it was actually an island, a large sandbank dotted with fishermen's cottages. Later, the narrow estuary of the River Bure at the northern end was blocked off, causing it to flow down the western side of the town. It runs parallel to the sea for two miles before joining the larger River Yare, and then their united waters curve around the southern edge of the town for another three miles before finally entering the sea.

So Yarmouth is now a promontory, its eastern and western sides displaying markedly different characters. The seaward side is a 5-mile stretch of sandy beaches and countless amusements, with a

Town Hall and Waterfront

breezy promenade from which one can watch the constant traffic of ships in Yarmouth Roads, and two fine old traditional piers, the Britannia (810ft long) and the Wellington (600ft). Of the host of entertainments on offer, three are particularly suitable for families. *The Sea Life Centre* includes displays of the kinds of marine life found on the Norfolk coast and an underwater viewing channel passing through shark-infested "oceans"; *Amazonia*, which is an indoor tropical paradise amongst whose reptilian residents are a 13ft alligator and a python which if fully uncoiled would extend to some

24ft; and the **Merrivale Model Village** which offers attractive land-scaped gardens, children's rides, and an exceptionally detailed miniature village with more than 200 models.

Also on the sea front are the **Maritime Museum of East Anglia**, housed in what was formerly the Shipwrecked Sailors' Home; the **Elizabethan House** (National Trust), a merchant's house of 1596, now a museum of domestic life with 16th century panelled rooms and a functional Victorian kitchen; and, behind South Beach, the 144ft high **Nelson's Monument** crowned by a statue, not of Norfolk's most famous son, but of Britannia. A sinew-stretching climb up the 217 steps to the viewing platform is rewarded by some striking views.

Most of Yarmouth's older buildings are concentrated in the western, or riverside, part of the town. Here you'll find **The Quay**, which Daniel Defoe considered the most beautiful in England, more than a mile long and in places 150 yards wide; a stately Town Hall worth visiting to see its grand staircase, Court Room and Assembly Room; and **The Rows**, a medieval network of tiny courtyards and narrow alleys, a mere two feet wide in places. The Rows were badly damaged during a bombing raid in 1942 but enough remains to show their unique character. There were originally 145 of these rows, about 7 miles in total, all of them built at right angles to the sea and therefore freely ventilated by onshore breezes which, given the urban sanitary conditions of those times, must have been extremely welcome.

The bombing raid of 1942 also completely destroyed the interior of **St Nicholas' Church**, but left its walls standing. Between 1957-60, this huge building - the largest parish church in England, was completely restored and furnished in traditional style largely by using pieces garnered from redundant churches and other sources. The partly Norman font, for example, came from Highway church in Wiltshire: the organ from St Mary-the-Boltons in Kensington.

Just south of the church, off the Market Place, is the half-timbered house, built in 1641, in which Anna Sewell lived. The author of "Black Beauty" was born in the town in 1820 but it was only when she was in her late 50s that she transmuted her concern for the more humane treatment of horses into a classic and seemingly timeless novel. Anna was paid just £20 for the rights to a book which, in the five months that elapsed between its publication and her death in 1878, had already sold an incredible 100,000 copies.

Another famous author associated with the town is Charles Dickens who stayed at the Royal Hotel on Marine Parade in 1847-48 while writing "David Copperfield". Dickens had visited the town as a child and had actually seen an upturned boat on the beach being used as a dwelling, complete with a chimney emerging from its keel. In his novel, this becomes Peggotty's house to which young Copperfield is brought following the death of his mother. *"One thing I particularly noticed in this delightful house"*, he writes, *"was the smell of fish; which was so searching, that when I took out my pocket-handkerchief to wipe my nose, I found it smelt exactly as if it had wrapped up a lobster"*.

In fact, the whole town at that time was pervaded with the aroma of smoked herrings, the silvery fish which were the basis of Yarmouth's prosperity. Around the time of Dickens' stay here, the author of the town's directory tried to pre-empt any discouraging effect this might have on visitors by claiming that *"The wholesome exhalations arising from the fish during the operation of curing are said to have a tendency to dissipate contagious disorders, and to be generally beneficial to the human constitution which is here sometimes preserved to extreme longevity"*.

Across the town, some 60 curing houses were busy gutting, salting and spicing herrings to produce Yarmouth's great contribution to the English breakfast, the kipper. The process had been invented by a Yarmouth man, John Woodger: a rival of his, a Mr Bishop, developed a different method which left the fish wonderfully moist and flavoursome, and so created the famous Yarmouth bloater.

For centuries, incredible quantities of herring were landed, nearly a billion in 1913 alone. In earlier years, the trade had involved so many fishermen that there were more boats (1,123) registered at Yarmouth than at London. But the scale of the over-fishing produced the inevitable result and suddenly, within the space of two decades, the 1950s and 1960s, Yarmouth's herring industry found itself dead in the water. Luckily, the end of that historic trade coincided with the beginning of North Sea oil and gas exploitation, a business which has kept the town in reasonably good economic health up to the present day.

Around Great Yarmouth

Burgh Castle   *Map 6 ref M7*
4 miles W of Great Yarmouth, on minor road off the A12 or A143
When the Romans established their fortress of *Garionnonum*, now known as Burgh Castle, the surrounding marshes were still under

water. The fort then stood on one bank of a vast estuary, commanding a strategic position at the head of an important waterway running
into the heart of East Anglia. The ruins are impressive, with walls
of alternating flint and brick layers rising 15ft high in places, and
spreading more than 11ft wide at their base. The Romans abandoned Garionnonum around AD 408 and some two centuries later
the Irish missionary St Fursey (or Fursa) founded a monastery
within its walls. Later generations cannibalised both his building,
and much of the crumbling Roman castle, as materials for their
own churches and houses.

Occupying a superb location near the church and castle, ***Church
Farm Free House*** overlooks the point where the Rivers Yare and
Waveney meet and flow into Breydon Water. From the dining-room
and balcony there are magical views across to the famous Berney
Arms Mill and the wetlands beyond. Felix Snall and Karen Webb
bought this 200 year-old Grade II listed farmhouse in 1988 and the
dozens of Commendations and Excellence Awards they have received
since then testify to their success in creating a first-class hostelry.

Inside, there's a wonderful old brick fireplace dated 1822, a tiny
snug with an original cast iron and tile fireplace, ancient bottles
and gleaming brassware everywhere and, an excellent amenity for
customers to bring their children, a separate café complete with
video games.

Fish dishes are the speciality here, but you'll also find a good
selection of meat and vegetarian options, along with a choice of wines

Church Farm Free House

and real ales to complement them. Church Farm is open all day, seven days a week, with food available every day from 12.00 to 15.00, and 18.00 to 22.00.

All but one of the 6 letting rooms at Church Farm are en suite, and for a rather special experience you should book the Honeymoon Room with its 4-poster bed and panoramic views across the Broads. *Church Farm Free House, Church Road, Burgh Castle, Great Yarmouth, NR31 9QG. Tel: 01493 780251*

Caister-on-Sea   Map 6 ref M6
4 miles N of Great Yarmouth, on the A149

In Boadicea's time, this modern holiday resort with its stretch of fine sands, was an important fishing port for her people, the Iceni. After the Romans had vanquished her unruly tribe, they settled here sometime in the 2nd century and built a "castra", or castle, or Caister, of which only a few foundations and remains have yet been found. **Caister Castle**, which stands in a picturesque setting about a mile to the west of the town, is a much later construction, built in 1432-5 by the legendary Sir John Fastolf with his spoils from the French wars in which he had served, very profitably, as Governor of Normandy and also distinguished himself leading the English bowmen at the Battle of Agincourt. Academics have enjoyed themselves for centuries disputing whether this Sir John was the model for Shakespeare's immortal rogue, Falstaff. Certainly, the historic Sir John was a larger-than-life character, but there's no evidence that he shared Falstaff's other characteristics of cowardliness, boastfulness and general over-indulgence.

Caister Castle was the first in England to be built of brick and is in fact one of the earliest brick buildings in the county. The 90ft tower remains, together with much of the moated wall and gatehouse, now lapped by still waters and with ivy relentlessly encroaching. The castle is open daily from May to September and, as an additional attraction, there is a Motor Museum in the grounds which houses an impressive collection of veteran, Edwardian, and vintage cars, an antique fire engine, and the original car used in the film of Ian Fleming's *Chitty Chitty Bang Bang*.

About 3 miles west of Caister Castle, the pleasantly landscaped grounds surrounding an 1876 Victorian mansion have been transformed into the **Thrigby Hall Wildlife Gardens**, home for a renowned collection of Asian mammals, birds and reptiles. There are snow leopards and rare tigers; gibbons and crocodiles; deer and otters; and other attractions include a tropical house, aviaries, waterfowl lake, willow pattern garden, gift shop and cafe. The Gardens are open every day, all year round.

Ormesby St Michael
Map 6 ref M5

9 miles NW of Great Yarmouth, on the A149

Just to the north of this tiny village, at Decoy Farm, is the **Norfolk Rare Breeds Centre**, home to a wide variety of domestic and rare breed farm animals enjoying a tranquil Broadland setting. Visitors can inspect the extensive collection of unusual species, see chicks hatching in the incubation room, wander round the museum which houses an interesting collection of old farm-carts, follow the Nature Trail, enjoy home-made cakes in the tearoom, and perhaps take a memento home from the well-stocked gift shop. Throughout the year, there are special events such as sheep shearing and a Heavy Horse Day. For more details, telephone 01493 732990.

Buckenham Ferry
Map 6 ref K7

13 miles W of Great Yarmouth, on minor road off the A146

Occupying a splendid position beside the River Yare, the **Beauchamp Arms** provides an excellent stopping-off place for travellers by both road and river. There are moorings for river craft, facilities for sailing and water-skiing are available, and this stretch

The Beauchamp Arms

of the river is a favourite with Yare anglers. (The catches here are good and there are frequent fishing matches for pike and bream). The Beauchamp Arms is also popular with bird-watchers visiting the RSPB sanctuary a couple of miles upstream.

The inn's owners, Ray and Maureen Hollocks, have two young children of their own, so young people are well-provided for, with their own room inside, and a play area outside, complete with bouncy castle. On fairweather days, grown-ups will appreciate the patio and attractive beer garden where they can enjoy one of Maureen's tasty bar meals alfresco. Maureen trained as a Cordon Bleu chef and her menu has a definite international flavour. There's a good choice of grills, steaks and chicken dishes, as well as freshly made pasta offerings.

The Beauchamp Arms' popularity is all the more striking since even large-scale maps don't mark Buckenham Ferry, and Buckenham itself is on the other side of the river. There are plans to re-instate the ferry which for centuries carried foot-travellers across the Yare at this point, but until then the best way to find this particular Hidden Place is either to arrive by river, or to take the A146 from Norwich towards Lowestoft, turn left after about 4 miles to Rockland St Mary, on to Claxton, and about 1 mile after Claxton, turn left on the No Through Road which will bring you after half a mile or so to the Beauchamp Arms. You'll be glad you took a little extra trouble seeking it out! *Beauchamp Arms, Buckenham Ferry, Langley, Norwich, NR14 6DH. Tel: 01508 480247*

The Norfolk Broads

If you want to experience a bird's-eye view which encompasses the essence of the Norfolk Broads, climb the tower of the *"Cathedral of the Broads"*, the **Church of St Helen's** at Ranworth. Spread out beneath you lies a vast panorama of glittering waterways, acres of marshland dotted with windmills, reed beds which are still harvested for thatch, grand medieval churches, and farmhouses of warm, red brick.

This is Britain's finest wetland area, a National Park in all but name, and although it's not entirely man-made, human exploitation has certainly played a large part in creating this unique landscape. From pre-Roman times, the people of Norfolk had dug peat from the marshes for fuel, (little usable timber was available in this soggy terrain). Over the centuries, the peat-digger's excavations left great trenches, 15ft deep in places. Then in the 14th century, the sea-level rose, the climate became wetter, and these huge pits filled with water, so forming the "broad" expanses of water from which the area takes its name.

Broadland covers some 220 square miles, in a rough oval to the northwest of Great Yarmouth. Three main rivers, the Ant, the Thurne, and the Bure, thread their way through the marshes, providing some 120 miles of navigable waterways. As mentioned earlier, the volume of tourist traffic has caused serious problems with pollution, erosion and silting, but recent measures will hopefully reverse these damaging effects. Despite the loss of once familiar sights such as the massive wild water-lily meadows, which have virtually disappeared, the Broads are still a refuge for many species of endangered birds and plants, and during the spring and autumn, they are a favourite stopping-off place for migrating birds.

Sadly, one rarely sees today the single-sailed boat, the wherry, which was once ubiquitous on the Broads. These barges with their shallow draughts and characteristic single black sail were specially designed for manoeuvrability on the windswept and often very shallow waters of the area. The wherries were the delivery vans of the pre-automobile age, travelling from one village "staithe", or quay, to another to off-load their cargoes of corn, coal, reed and sedge. Currently, a sole trading wherry still sails the Broads. It's named the *Albion*, is owned and sailed by the Norfolk Wherry Trust, and should you be lucky enough to see it gliding past, it makes a memorable picture.

This tour of the region starts at Acle, on the southern edge of the Broads, and travels more or less clockwise around the area, ending up at Norfolk's, and England's tallest windmill.

Acle   *Map 6 ref L6*
10 miles NW of Great Yarmouth, off the A47

A thousand years ago, this small market town, now 10 miles inland, was a small fishing port on the coast. Gradually, land has been reclaimed from the estuaries of the Rivers Bure, Waveney and Yare so that today large expanses of flat land stretch away from Acle towards the sea. The town's importance as a boating centre began in the 19th century with boat-building yards springing up beside the bridge. When Acle's first Regatta was held in 1890, some 150 yachts took part. The town became known as the "Gateway to the Broads" and also as the gateway to "Windmill Land", a picturesque stretch of the River Bure dotted with windmills. The medieval bridge that formerly crossed the Bure at Acle has less agreeable associations since it was used for numerous executions with the unfortunate victims left to dangle over the river.

Acle was granted permission for a market in 1272 and it's still held every Thursday, attracting visitors from miles around. Others come to see the unusual **Church of St Edmund** with its Saxon round tower, built some time around AD 900, crowned with a 15th century belfry from which eight carved figures look down on the beautifully thatched roof of the nave. The treasures inside include a superbly carved font, 6ft high, and inscribed with the date 1410, and a fine 15th century screen.

Located on the B1140 road from Acle to South Walsham, **Mannings Hotel & Restaurant** is a small commercial and well-balanced hotel, run in the best traditions of a family enterprise. There are extensive lawns to both the front and rear, a secluded and peaceful beer garden with an attractive fishpond feature, and a picnic area with tables and benches. Inside, the hotel has been recently refurbished to a very high standard and the 10 letting rooms are well-furnished and notably comfortable, with en suite bathrooms, colour television, telephone, clock radio and coffee-making facilities.

The restaurant is fully licensed and open to non-residents. Upholding the best traditions and the highest standards in catering, its cuisine has a good claim to being the best in the area. A full à la carte menu is offered every evening, with dishes prepared using only the freshest and finest quality fish, meat and vegetables. The menu provides a good choice of steaks, fish dishes (Tiger Prawns in

Mannings Hotel & Restaurant

filo pastry, perhaps), and poultry, and a selection of vegetarian dishes are available, made to order. Dinner is available every evening, and lunch on Sundays only, from 12 noon until 2pm. Both the restaurant and the spacious Bar Lounge enjoy pleasing views over the lawns at the front of the hotel.

Mannings Hotel, which enjoys an English Tourist Board rating of 3-Stars Commended, also offers special value-for-money weekend breaks which include breakfasts, dinner on Friday and Saturday, and Sunday lunch. The hotel is conveniently located close to some of the most attractive areas of the Broads, the manifold attractions of Norwich are less than a dozen miles away, while if you travel eastwards, the Bygone Heritage Museum at Burgh St Margaret, the Rare Breeds Farm at Ormesby St Margaret, and the east coast beaches are all within easy reach. *Mannings Hotel & Restaurant, South Walsham Road, Acle, NR13 3ES. Tel: 01493 750377/ Fax: 751220*

South Walsham *Map 6 ref L6*
9 miles E of Norwich, on the B1140

From Mannings Hotel, continue along the B1140 to South Walsham, a small village notable for having two parish churches built within yards of each other. In the heart of this Broadland village stands **The King's Arms**, and above its entrance is blazoned the motto: "Nous Sommes Ce Que Nous Mangeons", - "We are what we eat". Good food is certainly taken seriously at Mike Boning and Lynn

The King's Arms

Creasey's attractive old inn. Mike has been a contestant in the television programme *Masterchef,* and was a finalist in the Raymond Blanc Scholarship in 1996. Now he devotes his talents to creating first-class food for both his extensive à la carte menu and the bar menu. (Children too have their own selection of meals).

The King's Arms has 2 bars and a separate dining-room, each area boasting a different kind of striking fireplace. Dozens of vintage photographs of local people and places decorate the walls, along with interesting old collectables like the pictures of bygone footballers and cigarette packets from years ago. Outside, there's a patio and a peaceful covered area draped with vines. South Walsham's convenient location within a few miles of both Norwich and the glorious east coast beaches, and with the Norfolk Broads virtually on the doorstep, makes it an ideal place to stay. The King's Arms has 2 doubles and 1 twin room, all en suite, and all very comfortably appointed. And since any self-respecting old hostelry must have a resident ghost, the King's Arms goes one better by being host to two of them. One is a gentleman; the other a lady whom you'll recognise by her red dress and lace collar. *The King's Arms, Burlingham Road, South Walsham, NR13 6DJ. Tel: 01603 270039*

With its neatly thatched roof and walls of warm red brick, **Old Hall Farm** is the very picture of an inviting old Norfolk farmhouse. A major fire some years ago provided the opportunity for installing all modern amenities, such as central heating and double glazing, and the guest rooms were refurbished to a very high standard while maintaining the old house's period charm. Richard and Veronica

Old Hall Farm

Dewing now welcome bed and breakfast guests to their tastefully restored farmhouse set in its own extensive grounds. Richard has retired from farming, but still has three acres of land for growing vegetables and for his Free Range hens. And there are still cows belonging to a friend of the family to meet! Old Hall Farm has 3 guest rooms, (1 double, 1 twin and 1 single), all of them en suite. The Dewings offer a comprehensive breakfast, - good, wholesome food cooked on a wonderful tiled Aga, and will also provide packed lunches if ordered the previous evening. Please note that Old Hall Farm is a non-smoking house. *Old Hall Farm, South Walsham, NR13 6DT. Tel: 01603 270271*

Just to the north of the village is the ***Fairhaven Garden Trust***, an expanse of delightful water gardens lying beside the private ***South Walsham Inner Broad***. Its centrepiece is the 900 year old King Oak, lording it over the surrounding displays of rare shrubs and plants, native wildflowers, rhododendrons and giant lilies. There are tree-lined walks, a bird sanctuary, plants for sale, and a restaurant. A vintage style river boat runs trips every half-hour around the Broad. Tel: 01603 270449

The best way to see the remains of ***St Benet's Abbey*** is from a boat along the River Bure, (indeed it's quite difficult to reach it any other way). Rebuilt in 1020 by King Canute, after the Vikings had destroyed an earlier Saxon building, St Benet's became one of the richest abbeys in East Anglia. When Henry VIII closed it down in 1536 he made an unusual deal with its last Abbot. In return for creating the Abbot Bishop of Norwich, the Cathedral estates were to be handed over to the King but St Benet's properties could remain in the Abbot/Bishop's possession. Even today, the Bishop of Norwich retains the additional title of Abbot of St Benet's, and on the first Sunday in August each year, travels the last part of the journey by boat to hold an open-air service near the stately ruins of the Abbey gatehouse.

Ranworth   *Map 6 ref K5*
14 miles NW of Great Yarmouth, on minor road off the B1140
This beautiful Broadland village is famous for its church and its position on Ranworth Broad. From the tower of ***St Helen's Church*** it is possible to see 5 Norfolk Broads, Horsey Mill, the sea at Great Yarmouth, and on a clear day, the spire of Norwich Cathedral. Inside, the church houses one of Norfolk's greatest ecclesiastical treasures, a breathtaking early 15th century Gothic choir screen, the most beautiful and the best preserved in the county. In glowing

reds, greens and golds, gifted medieval artists painted a gallery of more than thirty saints and martyrs, inserting tiny cameos of such everyday scenes as falcons seizing hares, dogs chasing ducks and, oddly for Norfolk, lions. Cromwell's bigoted vandals, offended by such idolatrous images, smothered them with brown paint, - an ideal preservative for these wonderful paintings as became apparent when they were once again revealed during the course of a 19th century restoration of the church.

Just to the north of the village is the **Broadland Conservation Centre** (Norfolk Naturalists Trust), a thatched building floating on pontoons at the edge of Ranworth Broad. It houses an informative exhibition on the history of the Broads, and there's also an interesting Nature Trail which shows how these wetlands gradually developed over the centuries.

Horning   *Map 6 ref K5*
12 miles NE of Norwich, off the A1062

The travel writer Arthur Mee described Horning as *"Venice in Broadland"*, where *"waterways wandering from the river into the gardens are crossed by tiny bridges"*. With its pretty reed-thatched cottages lining the bank of the River Bure and its position in the heart of the Broads, there are few more attractive places from which to explore this magical area.

Located at the heart of this popular boating village is Joy Self's **Mill Crafts & Coffee Shop**. It stands right next to the village green, on the bank of the River Bure, and is conveniently placed for visitors arriving for, or from, river trips on the cruiser *Southern Comfort*. Joy's excellent Cream Teas are understandably very much in demand, and so too are the locally-baked cakes, scones and tea-cakes. The menu also includes a good choice of hot and cold food, - an all-day breakfast, omelettes, jacket potatoes and toasties, as well as ploughman's salads and filled rolls or sandwiches. There's a children choice (waffle & beans, perhaps) and the selection of beverages includes Norfolk apple juice and milk-shakes.

From the coffee shop, visitors can step straight into the Crafts shop where Joy offers a splendid array of quality hand-crafted gifts. There's everything from ceramics to cushions, candles to cards, along with jewellery, painted glass and works by local artists. A great place to browse and ideal if you are looking for a distinctive and attractive birthday or Christmas present. Horning village can also offer its visitors facilities for tennis, bowling and fishing, and the surrounding countryside is one of the most picturesque areas in

Mill Crafts & Coffee Shop

Broadland, where you can still see such traditional sights as peat-cutters at work and stacks of reeds piled alongside the waterways. *Mill Crafts & Coffee Shop, 12, Lower Street, Horning, NR12 8AA. Tel: 01692 631400*

Repps with Bastwick
Map 6 ref L5

12 miles NW of Great Yarmouth. off the A149

If you are looking for somewhere rather special to stay in this picturesque area, **Simon Stearn Holidays** offer an excellent choice of 10 different and very individual cottages set in one and a half acres of award-winning gardens near the little village of Repps. Backing onto grazing land, "Thurnefield" as the complex is called, enjoys a private setting at the end of a country lane, with the River Thurne just 100 yards away. Running through the heart of the Broads, the Thurne is a popular sailing and fishing river. Guests at "Thurnefield" bringing their own boat have use of the public slipway and free mooring, or hire of a day boat can be arranged through the owners. Other amenities available for all visitors are an outdoor swimming pool, (heated from mid-May to mid-September); a children's play area; and a barbecue.

A detailed brochure is available from Simon Stearn Holidays, but a few examples should help give an idea of the variety of accommodation available at "Thurnefield". Apple Tree Cottage (sleeps 4 + cot) and Cherry Tree Cottage (4 + cot, 4 + child) are two charming thatched, semi-detached cottages set in the centre of these lovely gardens. Special features include a bread oven in Cherry Tree, and

Simon Stearn Holidays

both cottages have lots of exposed beams. Harnser (4 + 2 children + cot) and Grebe (4 + cot) are two completely self-contained apartments on the ground floor of North End House, a barn-type conversion with beams and many leaded windows. Or you could choose one of the four small bungalow style cottages, all of which overlook open farmlands and spacious lawned gardens.

All the properties at "Thurnefield" are very well-appointed with all-electric amenities such as cooker, fridge, kettle, toaster, etc.: even an electric blanket on double beds for early and late bookings. Electricity is charged by meter reading. Each cottage is also provided with garden furniture and if you have a dog as part of the family, one large, or two small, canines can share your holiday on payment of a small additional charge. *Simon Stearn Holidays, Staithe Road, Repps with Bastwick, nr Potter Heigham, NR29 5JU. Tel: 01692 670320*

Potter Heigham   Map 6 ref L5
13 miles NW of Great Yarmouth, off the A149

Modern Potter Heigham has sprung up around the medieval bridge over the River Thurne, a low-arched structure with a clearance of only 7ft at its highest, a notorious test for novice sailors. The Thurne is a major artery through the Broads, linking them in a continuous waterway from Horsey Mere in the east to Wroxham Broad in the west. Generally regarded as one of the liveliest of the Broadland boating centres, Potter Heigham is also home to the **Museum of the Broads**, located in boat sheds in the historic Herbert Woods

Museum of the Broads

boat yard. Amongst the museum's many intriguing exhibits are the only concrete dinghy ever constructed; an ice yacht; tools from traditional Broads industries such as eel catching; gun punts for duck-shooting, complete with incredibly long guns; and a display featuring one of Broadland's most destructive pests, the coypu.

A pleasant excursion from Potter Heigham is a visit to **Horsey Mere**, about 6 miles to the east, and **Horsey Windpump** (both National Trust). From this early 20th century drainage mill, now restored and fully working, there are lovely views across the Mere. A circular walk follows the north side of Horsey Mere, passes another windmill, and returns through the village. There's a small shop at the Windpump, and light refreshments are available.

Wroxham
Map 6 ref K5

8 miles NE of Norwich, on the A1151

This riverside village, linked to its twin, Hoveton, by a hump-backed bridge over the River Bure, is the self-styled "capital" of the Norfolk Broads and as such, gets extremely busy during the season. The banks of the river are chock-a-block with boatyards full of cruisers of all shapes and sizes, there's a constant traffic of boats making their way to the open spaces of **Wroxham Broad**, and in July the scene becomes even more hectic when the annual Regatta is under way.

Wroxham is also the southern terminus of the **Bure Valley Railway**, a 9-mile long, narrow-gauge (15") steam train service that closely follows the course of the River Bure through lovely country-side to the market town of Aylsham. It runs along the trackbed of the old East Norfolk Railway, has 2 half-scale locomotives, and spe-cially constructed passenger coaches with large windows to provide the best possible views. In the high season, there are half a dozen trains each day, in both directions, and throughout the year there are special events such as the "Friends of Thomas the Tank Engine" days, and "Santa Specials". And if you still cherish that childhood ambition of becoming a train driver, the BVR also runs one- or two-day Steam Driving Courses, framed to suit anyone from the abso-lute beginner upwards. More details of these, and the timetable, on 01263 733858.

A couple of miles north of Wroxham is **Wroxham Barns**, a de-lightful collection of beautifully restored 18th century barns, set in 10 acres of countryside, and housing a community of craftspeople. There are thirteen of them, producing between them a wide range of crafts, from stained glass to woodturning, stitchcraft to hand-made children's clothes, pottery to floral artistry, and much more. The complex also includes a cider-pressing centre; a junior farm with lots of "hands on" activities; a traditional Family Fair (with individually priced rides); a Gift & Craft Shop; and a tearoom. Open daily all year. For more details, call 01603 783762.

A mile or so east of Wroxham Barns, **Hoveton Hall Gardens** offer visitors a splendid combination of plants, shrubs and trees, with rare rhododendrons, azaleas, water plants, and dazzling her-baceous borders within a walled garden. There are woodland and lakeside walks, plant sales, gardening books, and a tea room. For opening times, call 01603 782798.

Anyone interested in dried flower arrangements should make their way to the tiny hamlet of Cangate, another couple of miles to the east, where **Willow Farm Flowers** provides an opportunity of seeing the whole process, from the flowers in the field to the final colourful displays. The farm shop has an abundance of dried, silk, parchment and wooden flowers, beautifully arranged, and more than 50 varieties of dried flowers are available in bunches or made into arrangements of all shapes and sizes, or to special order. Willow Farm also has a picnic and play area, a guided farm walk, lays on flower arranging demonstrations and also runs one day classes for those interested in learning more about mastering this delicate-fin-gered skill. For further details, telephone 01603 783588.

Hoveton St John

Map 6 ref K5

9 miles NE of Norwich, on the A1151

The Black Horse at Hoveton St John takes its name from the nearby Black Horse Broad, (also known as Hoveton Little Broad), a peaceful 60-acre expanse where pleasure craft are banned and waterfowl abound. From the outside, Valerie Pleydell's hostelry has an inviting appearance, with its many hanging baskets and tubs filled with flowers, and inside there's a genuinely warm welcome. The Black

The Black Horse

Horse is a free house with most of its ales coming from Suffolk's oldest brewery, Adnam's Sole Bay brewery. In the separate light and airy dining room, blackboards display the bill of fare. Almost everything listed is home-made, most notably the pies, (Rabbit for your main meal, perhaps, with Bramley Apple pie to follow?). Food can be enjoyed either in the restaurant, or outside where there's also a children's play area. The Black Horse has good wheelchair access and, a rather unusual feature, its "Front Room" bar is called that because it resembles the front room of a private house with its soft sofas and little knick-knacks all around. *The Black Horse, Horning Road, Hoveton St John, Norwich, NR12 8JN. Tel: 01692 630271*

Coltishall

Map 6 ref J5

8 miles N of Norwich, on the B1150/B1354

This charming village beside the River Bure captivates visitors with its riverside setting, leafy lanes, elegant Dutch-gabled houses, village green and thatched church. Coltishall has a good claim to its title of "Gateway to Broadland" since for most cruisers this is the beginning of the navigable portion of the Bure. Anyone interested in Norfolk's industrial heritage will want to seek out the ***Ancient Lime Kiln***, next door to the Railway Tavern in Station Road. Lime, formerly an important part of Norfolk's rural economy, is obtained by heating chalk to a very high temperature in a kiln. Most of the county sits on a bed of chalk, but in the area around Coltishall and Horstead it is of a particularly high quality. The kiln at Coltishall, one of the few surviving in the country, is a listed building of finely finished brickwork, built in a style unique to Norfolk.

The top of the tapered kiln pot is level with the ground, and down below a vaulted walkway allowed access to the grills through which the lime was raked out. This was uncomfortable and even danger-ous work since fresh lime, when it comes into contact with a moist surface, such as a human body, becomes burning hot. The lime had to be slaked with water before it could be used as a fertiliser, for mortar or as whitewash. Access to the kiln is by way of the Railway Tavern, but during the months from October to March you may find that the building has been taken over by a colony of hibernating bats which, by law, may not be disturbed. In which case, settle for a drink and/or meal in the Railway Tavern which has an historic in-terest of its own, dating back as it does to 1687. Clem and Ann, the owners of this friendly pub set in 2 acres of its own grounds, also run a rescue home for unwanted animals, amongst them donkeys, rabbits and guinea pigs. Injured seagulls, ducks and swans are of-ten taken in and cared for until they are well enough to be released.

A couple of miles south of Coltishall, on the B1150, is another animal refuge, the ***Redwings Horse Sanctuary***, founded in 1984 to provide a caring and permanent home for horses, ponies, don-keys and mules rescued from neglect and slaughter. The Sanctuary cares for more than 1000 animals at any one time, and there are no indications that this number is likely to diminish. Even with the help of many volunteers, the work is expensive. To raise funds, the Sanctuary holds Open Days every Sunday and Bank Holiday after-noon from Easter to December, has a Gift Shop with many horse-related items on sale, and also runs an Adopt-a-Horse scheme. For more details, telephone 01603 737432.

Scottow   *Map 6 ref K4*
9 miles NE of Norwich, on the B1150

A charming sight with its pink-washed walls, thatched roof and masses of hanging-baskets, ***The Three Horseshoes*** is also a wel-

The Three Horseshoes

come sight for anyone who cherishes good food and real ale. This Grade II listed building goes back to the 17th century and it was the favourite pub of the famous World War II fighter pilot, Douglas Bader, when he was serving at the RAF base at Coltishall, a few miles down the road. That tradition has continued with the present generation of servicemen stationed at RAF Coltishall who are drawn here by The Three Horseshoe's outstanding food and carefully tended real ales. Richard and Joanne Brown are your hosts, with Richard in charge of the kitchen.

All the food is freshly prepared, so if you choose one of Richard's home-made pies or puddings, you are asked to allow at least 30 minutes for it to be served. They are well worth the wait, with a choice that includes Salmon & Prawn, Game Pie, and a hearty Steak & Kidney Pudding described as being "for the very hungry!" The excellent menu also includes some tasty starters, "sizzlers" such as Cajun Chicken or Cantonese Style Prawns; fish, chicken and steak dishes, as well as vegetarian options. Adjacent to the pub, the Long Barn that once served as a cow-shed, is now the Long Bar, an attractive room with an open fire at each end which can also be rented as a Function Room. *The Three Horseshoes, North Walsham Road, Scottow, NR10 5BZ. Tel: 01692 538243*

Worstead   *Map 6 ref K4*
12 miles NE of Norwich, on minor road off the A149 or B1150
Hard to imagine now, but Worstead was a busy little industrial centre in the Middle Ages. The village lent its name to the hard-wearing

cloth produced in the region, and many of the original weavers' cottages can still be seen in the narrow side-streets. Worsted cloth, woven from tightly-twisted yarn, was introduced by Flemish immigrants and became popular throughout England from the 13th century onwards. The Flemish weavers settled happily into the East Anglian way of life and seem to have influenced its architecture almost as strongly as its weaving industry.

The lovely 14th century **Church of St Mary** provides ample evidence of Worstead's former prosperity. Its many treasures include a fine hammerbeam roof, a chancel screen with a remarkable painted dado, and a magnificent traceried font complete with cover. The village stages an annual weekend of events to raise money for the restoration of the church and the memory of Worstead's days of glory is kept alive by a still-functioning Guild of Weavers. The Guild has placed looms in the north aisle of St Mary's, and from time to time there are demonstrations of the ancient skill of weaving.

North Walsham   *Map 6 ref K3*
9 miles SE of Cromer, on the A149

This busy country town with its attractive **Market Cross** of 1600 has some interesting historical associations. Back in 1381, despite its remoteness from London, North Walsham became the focus of an uprising in support of Wat Tyler's Peasants' Rebellion. These North Norfolk rebels were led by John Litester, a local dyer, and their object was the abolition of serfdom. Their actions were mainly symbolic: invading manor houses, monasteries and town halls and burning the documents that recorded their subservient status. In a mass demonstration they gathered on Mousehold Heath outside Norwich, presented a petition to the King, and then retreated to North Walsham to await his answer. It came in the form of the sanguinary Bishop of Norwich, Henry Despenser, who, as his admiring biographer recorded, led an assault on the rebels, *"grinding his teeth like a wild boar, and sparing neither himself nor his enemies,....stabbing some, unhorsing others, hacking and hewing"*. John Litester was captured, summarily executed and, on the orders of the Bishop, "divided into four parts, and sent throughout the country to Norwich, Yarmouth, Lynn and to the site of his own house".

A more glorious fate awaited the town's most famous resident, Horatio Nelson, who came to the Paston School here in 1768 as a boy of ten. Horatio was already dreaming of a naval career and three years later, when he read in the county newspaper that his Uncle Maurice had been appointed commander of a warship, he prevailed on his father to let him join the *Raisonnable*.

The Paston School had been founded in 1606 by Sir William Paston. His ancestors were the writers of the extraordinary collection of more than a thousand letters, written between 1422 and 1509, which present an astonishingly vivid picture of East Anglian life at the end of the turbulent Middle Ages. Sir William himself is buried in the parish church where he personally supervised (and paid for) the construction of the impressive marble and alabaster monument he desired to be erected in his memory.

In the heart of the town, close to the church, is ***Butterfingers Tea Room***, owned and run by Maureen Larssen. Although Maureen only took over the tea room on April Fools' Day, 1997, the excellent fare on offer has made Butterfingers a highly popular place of resort and Maureen herself, who hails from Sunderland, has quickly been adopted as "one of the locals". The old red brick building still has its original flagged floor, with stones of every size, shape and colour. An interesting feature is an ancient baker's oven, and there are vintage photographs of the town hung around the walls, amongst them a striking one of the blacksmith Ernest Edward whose smithy used to operate in the Mitre Tavern Yard. The Butterfingers menu caters for all tastes and appetites. Breakfast comes in two sizes, large or small, and with two options, "veggie" or non-veggie. There's an extensive choice of light snacks, jacket potatoes, salads, sandwiches (regular, Club or toasted), and filled baps, all at extremely

Butterfingers Tea Room

The Hidden Places of Norfolk

reasonable prices. Not to be missed are the specialities of the house, Maureen's home made scones, (four varieties, cheese & chives being particularly tasty), and her wonderful cakes which are listed on the blackboard. Butterfingers is an exceptional tea room, a hidden place you should definitely seek out. *Butterfingers Tea Room, 1, Mitre Tavern Yard, North Walsham, NR28 9BN. Tel: 01692 500642*

Also just a short walk from the splendid church, **The Dutch Oven** is well-known locally as a high class bakery, confectionery and for its fresh wholesome food. It's a family business, run by Lewis Williams and his son, Christopher, who have been here since 1988 and have built up an impressive reputation for their devotion to customer care. The Dutch Oven has become something of a meeting place for local people but visitors will find themselves very welcome.

The menu offers a good choice of light meals and snacks from a hearty breakfast, through good old-fashioned Fish & Chips to a simple Egg on Toast. Sandwiches, filled rolls *The Dutch Oven* or jacket potatoes, ploughmans and salads all feature on the extensive menu. The single storey building has well-spaced tables and is able to accommodate the disabled. Parking is available about 75 yards away. The Dutch Oven's convenient town centre location makes it ideal when you need a refreshment break from shopping or sight-seeing. *The Dutch Oven, 4, Church Street, North Walsham, NR28 9DA. Tel: 01692 405955*

About 4 miles east of North Walsham, near the village of Erpingham on the A140, **Alby Crafts & Gardens** has a Crafts Gallery promoting the excellence of mainly East Anglian and British craftsmanship, - lacework, woodturning, jewellery, canework, and much more. The "Plantsman's Garden" displays a fine collection of unusual shrubs, plants and bulbs in a 4 acre site, there are workshops where you can watch craftsmen at work, a Bottle Museum, (small charge for admission), and a tea-room. For more details, call 01263 761590.

Mundesley   Map3 ref K2
7 miles SE of Cromer, on the B1159
"The finest air in the kingdom has been wasted for centuries" said a speaker celebrating the arrival of the railway at Mundesley in 1898, *"because nobody had the courage to bring the people to the district".*

The railway has been and gone, but the fresh breezes off the North Sea remain as invigorating as ever.

After the hazards of the coastline immediately to the north where cliffs, fields and houses have all been eroded by the relentless sea, it's a pleasure to arrive at this unassuming holiday resort with its superb sandy beach, considered by many the very best in Norfolk. Mundesley village is quite small (appropriately, its Maritime Museum is believed to the smallest museum in the country) but it provides all the facilities conducive to a relaxing family holiday. Best of all, there is safe swimming in the sea and when the tide is out children can spend many a happy hour exploring the many "lowes", or shallow lagoons, left behind.

Located, very appropriately in the heart of "Poppyland", is the *Overstrand Cottage Garden Centre*, a family business run by Derek and Sheila Smeda, their daughter and son-in-law. The Smeda family have owned the Centre for some six years now and its reputation is second to none in north-east Norfolk for the comprehensive range of plants, shrubs and trees on offer, as well as every possible

Overstrand Cottage Garden Centre

gardening aid you can think of. The one-acre site includes a pleasant refreshment room called, naturally, the "Poppyland Tea Room". The name was given to the area by a well-known Victorian journalist, Clement Scott. In 1883, he travelled to Cromer on the newly-opened Great Eastern Railway's extension from Norwich. Walking out of the town, he was entranced by the tranquillity of the countryside. In his despatch to the *Daily Telegraph* he wrote: *"It is difficult to convey an idea of the silence of the fields through which I passed, or the beauty of the prospect that surrounded me - a blue sky without a cloud across it, a sea sparkling under a haze of heat, wild flowers in profusion around me, poppies predominating every-where..."* Spurred by Scott's enthusiasm, a succession of notable Victorians made their way here, - painters, writers, actors, even a youthful Winston Churchill. Later, during World War II, Churchill returned to the area, staying at Pear Tree Cottage, just along the lane from the Smedas' Garden Centre. *Overstrand Cottage Garden Centre, Overstrand Road, Mundesley, nr Cromer, NR27 0PU. Tel: 01263 579485*

Paston
Map 3 ref K3
9 miles SE of Cromer, on the B1159

It was in this small village that the Paston family entered the historical record. The vivid collection of letters they wrote to each other during the years that England was being wracked by the Wars of the Roses has already been mentioned, and the village boasts another magnificent legacy from this remarkable family. In 1581, Sir William Paston built a cavernous tithe-barn here with flint walls and a thatched roof. It still stands, it's roof still thatched: 160ft long, almost 60ft high, - the longest, most imposing barn in Norfolk. In the nearby church, the most striking of the family memorials is the one dedicated to Katherine Paston. Sculpted in alabaster by Nicholas Stone in 1628, Katherine lies dressed to kill in her Jacobean finery of starched ruff, embroidered bodice, puffed sleeves and pearl neck-laces. The monument cost £340, a staggering sum of money at that time.

Bacton
Map 3 ref K3
11 miles SE of Cromer, on the B1159/B1150

A few miles south of Mundesley, Bacton has a hill-top church, a short sea-front and miles of wide sandy beaches. Occupying a fa-voured position just 100 yards from the water's edge, **The Ship Freehouse & Restaurant** is a spacious Victorian building with two bars and a separate restaurant. Its new owners, Bruce and Judy Barton, and Mary and Paul Quinn, only took over here in 1998 but word has spread quickly about the high quality of the food and ales on offer. The Ship serves 2 real ales as well as a comprehensive selection of all the usual favourite tipples. The menu draws heavily on local, fresh produce and includes an excellent choice of starters, grills, chicken and fish dishes, as well as vegetarian options and children's specials. The half-a-dozen sweets listed are supplemented by further choices on the Daily Specials Menu and, if you are taking wine with your meal, you will find a short but surprisingly varied

The Ship Freehouse and Restaurant

list to choose from. Should you be planning to stay in the area, The Ship can offer you accommodation, and the inn is also licensed as a Touring Caravan Site for which there is ample space. The beach nearby is of course one of Bacton's principal attractions, with wide stretches of sand, but a short walk will also take you to the ruins of Bromholm Priory, and a brief drive brings you to the historic houses of Felbrigg Hall and Blickling Hall, or to the picturesque Broads country just a few miles to the south. *The Ship Freehouse & Restaurant, Coast Road, Bacton, NR12 0EW. Tel: 01692 650420*

Happisburgh
Map 6 ref L3
14 miles SE of Cromer, on the B1159

The coastal waters off Happisburgh, (or "Hazeborough" to give the village its unlikely but correct pronunciation), have seen many a shipwreck over the centuries, and the victims lie buried in the grave-yard of **St Mary's Church**. The large grassy mound on the north side of the church contains the bodies of the ill-fated crew of *HMS Invincible*, wrecked on the treacherous sandbanks here in 1801. The ship was on its way to join up with Nelson's fleet at Copenhagen when the tragedy occurred, resulting in the deaths of 119 sailors. Happisburgh's distinctive Lighthouse, built in 1791 and striped like a barber's pole, certainly proved ineffectual on that occasion; as did the soaring 110ft tower of the church itself which could normally be relied on as a "back-up" warning to mariners.

Inside the Church is a splendid 15th century octagonal font carved with the figures of lions, satyrs, and "wild men"; and embedded in the pillars along the aisle are the marks left by shrapnel from German bombs dropped on the village in 1940.

Lessingham   *Map 6 ref L3*
17 miles SE of Cromer, off the B1159

From this small village a lane winds down through spectacular dunes to the sands at Eccles Beach and, a little further north, to Cart Gap with its gently sloping beach and colourful lines of beach huts.

Dating back to the 18th century, **The Star Inn** is very much a social centre for Lessingham village, even acting as the local Post Office. Peter and Jean Harrison have been here since 1992, but they have both been in the business for many years, Peter working for a brewery for some 25 years. Games are popular at The Star with pool, darts, and shove-halfpenny all available, and there's also a very active cribbage league. To the rear of the inn is the restaurant, attractively furnished and decorated in traditional style, where you'll find a good choice of fish, meat and vegetarian dishes, as well as children's meals, specials served to order (such as home-made lasagna), and desserts of the day which are listed on the boards. Locally-caught fish, too, will be listed here when it's available. The Roast Dinner on Sundays should definitely not be missed. In the bar itself, the menu of snacks and sandwiches represents very good value for money and on fine weather days you can enjoy your food

The Star Inn

outside, either on the patio area or in the garden. An additional amenity at The Star is its 3½ acres of grounds which are available for campers and caravanners. During the summer, Caravan Rallies can be held here, if booked early. *The Star Inn, School Road, Lessingham, NR12 0DN. Tel: 01692 580510*

About 4 miles south of Lessingham stands a windmill that is not just the tallest in Norfolk, but in the whole of England. Eighty feet high, **Sutton Windmill** was built in the year of the French Revolution, 1789, and its millstones only finally ground to a halt in 1940. Chris Nunn bought the mill in 1976 and since then he has devoted himself to renovating this glorious 9-storey building with the ultimate aim of restoring it to working order. During those years, Chris and his family have also built up a fascinating private collection of artefacts which reflect the social history of Norfolk over the past 150 years or so. These are on display in the family's privately-owned Broadlands Museum, a magpie's nest in which you'll find anything from vintage kitchen and veterinary tools to a reconstructed Pharmacy Shop of the 1880s, complete with a fine collection of patent medicines, ointments and pills. With its all-embracing portrait of Norfolk life, the **Broadlands Museum** seems a good place to conclude this tour of one of England's most enchanting counties.

Tourist Information Centres

Centres in **bold** are open all the year around.

Aylsham
Bure Valley Railway Station, Norwich Road, Aylsham
NR11 6BW   Tel: 01263 733903 Fax: 01263 733814

Cromer
Cromer Bus Station, Prince of Wales Road, Cromer, NR27 9HS
Tel: 01263 512497

Diss
The Meresmouth, Mere Street, Diss, IP22 3AG
Tel: 01379 650523 Fax: 01379 650838

Fakenham
Red Lion House, Market Place, Fakenham, NR21 9BY
Tel: 01328 851981

Great Yarmouth
Marine Parade, Great Yarmouth, NR30 2EJ
Tel: 01493 842195/846345

Hoveton
Station Road, Hoveton, NR12 8EU
Tel/Fax: 01603 782281

Hunstanton
Town Hall, The Green, Hunstanton, PE36 5BQ
Tel: 01485 532610 Fax: 01485 533972

King's Lynn

The Old Gaol House, Saturday Market Place, King's Lynn
PE30 5DQ   Tel: 01553 763044 Fax: 01553 777281

Mundesley

2 Station Road, Mundesley, NR11 8JH
Tel: 01263 721070

Norwich

The Guildhall, Gaol Hill, Norwich, NR2 1NF
Tel: 01603 666071 Fax: 01603 765389

Sheringham

Station Approach, Sheringham, NR26 8RA
Tel: 01263 824329

Walsingham

Common Place, Little Walsingham, NR22 6BP
Tel: 01328 820510

Wells-next-the-Sea

Staithe Street, Wells-next-the-Sea, NR23 1AN
Tel: 01328 710885

Index

The Hidden Places Series

ORDER FORM

To order more copies of this title or any of the others in this series
please complete the order form below and send to:

**Travel Publishing Ltd,7a Apollo House, Calleva Park
Aldermaston, Berks, RG7 8TN**

	Price	Quantity	Value
Regional Titles			
Channel Islands	£6.99	....	....
Cheshire	£7.99	....	....
Cornwall	£7.99	....	....
Devon	£7.99	....	....
Dorset, Hants & Isle of Wight	£4.95	....	....
Gloucestershire	£6.99	....	....
Heart of England	£4.95	....	....
Kent	£7.99	....	....
Lancashire	£7.99	....	....
Lake District & Cumbria	£7.99	....	....
Norfolk	£7.99	....	....
Northeast Yorkshire	£6.99	....	....
Northumberland & Durham	£6.99	....	....
Nottinghamshire	£6.99	....	....
Peak District	£6.99	....	....
Potteries	£6.99	....	....
Somerset	£6.99	....	....
South East	£4.95	....	....
South Wales	£4.95	....	....
Suffolk	£7.99	....	....
Surrey	£6.99	....	....
Sussex	£6.99	....	....
Thames & Chilterns	£5.99	....	....
Welsh Borders	£5.99	....	....
Wiltshire	£6.99	....	....
Yorkshire Dales	£6.99	....	....
Set of any 5 Regional titles £25.00		....	....
National Titles			
England	£9.99	....	....
Ireland	£8.99	....	....
Scotland	£8.99	....	....
Wales	£8.99	....	....
Set of all 4 National titles £28.00		....	....

TOTAL

**For orders of less than 4 copies please add £1 per book for
postage & packing. Orders over 4 copies P & P free.**

*PLEASE TURN OVER TO COMPLETE
PAYMENT DETAILS*

The Hidden Places Series
ORDER FORM

Please complete following details:

I wish to pay for this order by:

Cheque: ☐   Switch: ☐

Access: ☐   Visa: ☐

Either:

Card No: ☐☐☐☐ ☐☐☐☐ ☐☐☐☐ ☐☐☐☐

Expiry Date: ☐☐ ☐☐

Signature: ....

Or:

I enclose a cheque for £ .... made payable to Travel Publishing Ltd

NAME: ....

ADDRESS: ....

....

....

....

POSTCODE: ....

TEL NO: ....

Please send to: Travel Publishing Ltd
7a Apollo House
Calleva Park
Aldermaston
Berks, RG7 8TN

The Hidden Places Series
READER REACTION FORM

The Hidden Places research team would like to receive reader's comments on any visitor attractions or places reviewed in the book and also recommendations for suitable entries to be included in the next edition. This will help ensure that the *Hidden Places* series continues to provide its readers with useful information on the more interesting, unusual or unique features of each attraction or place ensuring that their stay in the local area is an enjoyable and stimulating experience.

To provide your comments or recommendations would you please complete the forms below as indicated and send to: **The Research Department, Travel Publishing Ltd., 7a Apollo House, Calleva Park, Aldermaston, Reading, RG7 8TN.**

Please tick as appropriate: Comments ☐   Recommendation ☐

Name of *"Hidden Place"*:

Address:

Telephone Number:

Name of Contact:

Comments/Reason for recommendation:

Name of Reader:

Address:

Telephone Number:

The Hidden Places Series
READER REACTION FORM

The Hidden Places research team would like to receive reader's comments on any visitor attractions or places reviewed in the book and also recommendations for suitable entries to be included in the next edition. This will help ensure that the **Hidden Places** series continues to provide its readers with useful information on the more interesting, unusual or unique features of each attraction or place ensuring that their stay in the local area is an enjoyable and stimulating experience.

To provide your comments or recommendations would you please complete the forms below as indicated and send to: **The Research Department, Travel Publishing Ltd., 7a Apollo House, Calleva Park, Aldermaston, Reading, RG7 8TN.**

Please tick as appropriate: Comments ☐ Recommendation ☐

Name of *"Hidden Place"*:

Address:

Telephone Number:

Name of Contact:

Comments/Reason for recommendation:

Name of Reader:

Address:

Telephone Number:

The Hidden Places Series
READER REACTION FORM

The Hidden Places research team would like to receive reader's comments on any visitor attractions or places reviewed in the book and also recommendations for suitable entries to be included in the next edition. This will help ensure that the ***Hidden Places*** series continues to provide its readers with useful information on the more interesting, unusual or unique features of each attraction or place ensuring that their stay in the local area is an enjoyable and stimulating experience.

To provide your comments or recommendations would you please complete the forms below as indicated and send to: **The Research Department, Travel Publishing Ltd., 7a Apollo House, Calleva Park, Aldermaston, Reading, RG7 8TN.**

Please tick as appropriate: Comments ☐   Recommendation ☐

Name of *"Hidden Place"*:

Address:

Telephone Number:

Name of Contact:

Comments/Reason for recommendation:

Name of Reader:

Address:

Telephone Number:

Map Section

The following pages of maps encompass the main cities, towns and geographical features of Norfolk as well as all the many interesting places featured in the guide. Distances are indicated by the use of scale bars located below each of the maps

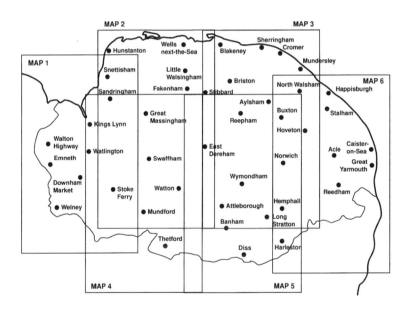

These maps are small scale extracts from the *East Anglia Official Tourist Map,* reproduced with kind permission of *Estates Publications.*

MAP 1

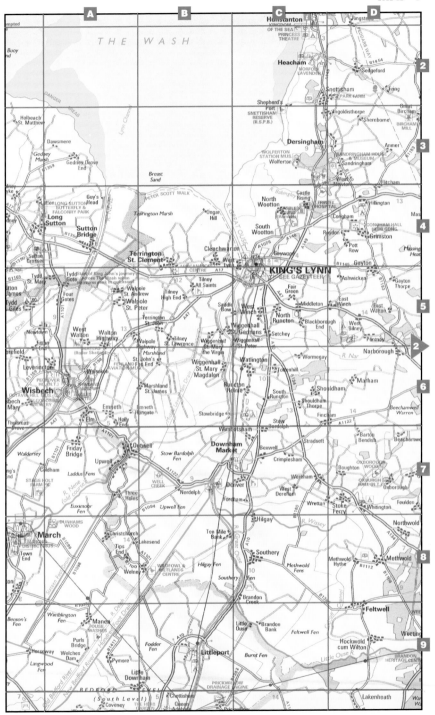

THE WASH

Hunstanton
KINGDOM OF THE SEA
PRINCESS THEATRE

Heacham
MORFOLK LAVENDER

Ringstead

PEDDARS WAY

Sedgeford

Fring

Shepherd's
Port
SNETTISHAM
RESERVE
(R.S.P.B.)

Snettisham
PARK FARM

Ingoldisthorpe

Shernborne

Great
Bircham

BIRCHAM
MILL

Anmer

Holbeach
St. Matthew

Dawsmere

Gedney
Marsh

Gedney Drove
End

Breast
Sand

Dersingham

WOLFERTON
STATION MUS
Wolferton

SANDRINGHAM HOUSE &
MUSEUM
Sandringham

West
Newton

Fitcham

Ilsington

Congham

Massi

Buoy
nd

DANGER
AREAS

Lynn Channel

PETER SCOTT WALK

Long Sutton
LONG SUTTON
BUTTERFLY &
FALCONRY PARK

Guy's
Head

Terrington Marsh

Ongar
Hill

North
Wootton

Castle
Rising
CASTLE
RISING
Roman Remains

TRINITY
HOSPITAL

CONGHAM HALL
HERB GDNS

Grimston

Sutton
Bridge

South
Wootton

Reydon

Pott
Row

Gayton

Massing
Hea

Sutton
Crosse

Terrington
St. Clement

Clenchwarton

West

KING'S LYNN
SEE GAZETTEER

Gaywood

Tydd
St. Mary

Tydd
Gote

Four
Gotes

Tilney
All Saints

Fair
Green

Ashwicken

Gayton
Thorpe

utton
ames

Tydd
St.
Giles

Walpole
St. Andrew

Walpole
St. Peter

Tilney
High End

Saddle
Bow

West
Winch

North
Runcton

Middleton

East
Winch

Blackborough
End

East
Walton

West
Bilney

West
Walton

Walton
Highway

Terrington
St. John

Tilney
St. Lawrence

Wiggenhall
St. Germans

Wiggenhall
St. Peter

Setchey

Pentney

Newtown

Narborough

R. Nar

Leverington

Walsoken

Walpole
Highway

Marshland
St. John's
FENLAND FEN END
AVIATION MUS

Wiggenhall
St. Mary
the Virgin

Watlington

Wormegay

Marham

Wisbech
St
Mary

OCTAVIA HILL BIRTHPLACE
HERITAGE CENTRE
WISBECH
& FENLAND MUSEUM
MUSEUM

Marshland
St. James

Wiggenhall
St. Mary
Magdalen

Runcton
Holme

Tottenhill

Shouldham

Beechamwell
Warren

Emneth

Emneth
Hungate

Elm

Holly
End

Stowbridge

South
Runcton

Shouldham
Thorpe

Finching

Stow
Bardolph

Barton
Bendish

Beachamw

Waldersey

Friday
Bridge

Upwell

Coldham

Outwell

Stow Bardolph
Fen

Downham
Market

Bexwell

Crimplesham

Stradsett

Boughton

OXBOROUGH
WOOD

OXBURGH
HALL (N.T.)

Oxborough

Laddus Fens

WELL
CREEK

Nordelph

Denver

West
Dereham

Wereham

Foulden

Three
Holes

Upwell Fen

Fordham

Wretton

Stoke
Ferry

Whittington

Euxmoor
Fen

DUNHAMS
WOOD

Christchurch

Lakesend

Ten Mile
Bank

Hilgay

R. Wissey

Northwold

March

TOWN
DISTRIBUTORS

Town
End

Tips
End

Welney

WILDFOWL &
WETLANDS
CENTRE

Hilgay Fen

Southery

Southery
Fen

Methwold
Fens

Methwold
Hythe

Methwold

Feltwell

Benson's
Fen

Wimblington
Fen

MANEA
HOUSE
WASHES

Purls
Bridge

Welches
Dam

Horseway

Manea

Pymore

Little
Downham

Fodder
Fen

Brandon
Creek

Little
Ouse

Brandon
Bank

Feltwell Fen

Hockwold
cum Wilton

Weeting

BRANDON
HERITAGE CENT

Littleport

Burnt Fen

Little Ouse R

Langwood
Fen

BEDFORD LEVEL

(South Level)

Coveney

Chettisham

PRICKWILLOW
DRAINAGE
ENGINE

Lakenheath

War

0 1 2 3 4 5 miles
0 1 2 3 4 5 6 7 8 kilometres

MAP 2

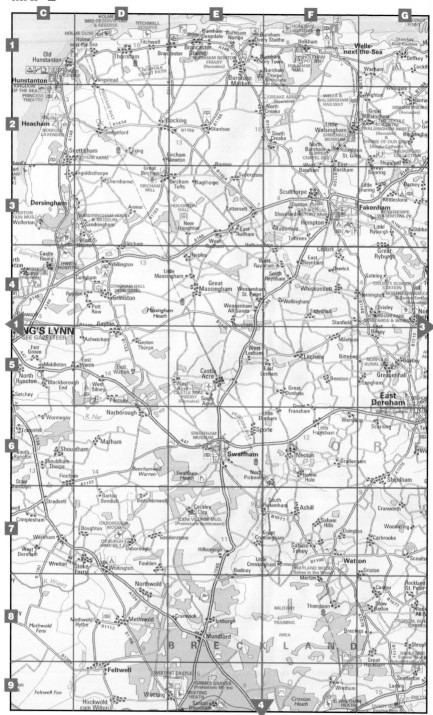

©Estate Publications   Crown Copyright Reserved

MAP 3

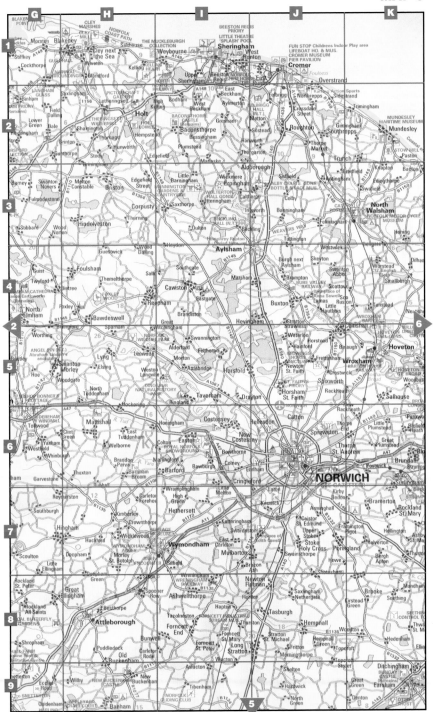

MAP 4

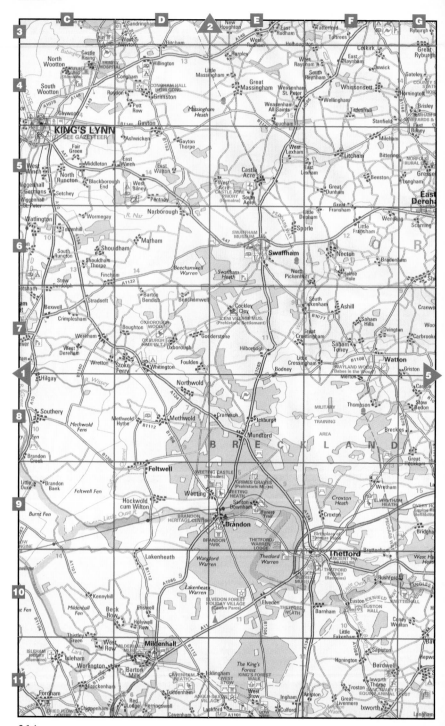

214

MAP 5

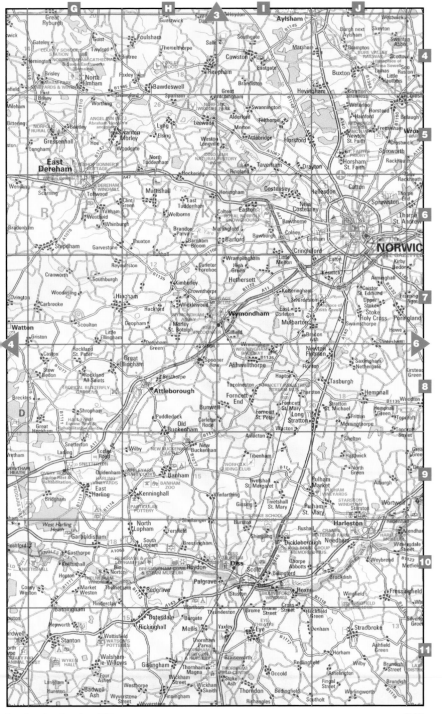

MAP 6

©Estate Publications   Crown Copyright Reserved